DATE DUE

DEMCO 38-296

Exploring Diversity
Literature Themes and Activities
for Grades 4-8

Jean E. Brown
Elaine C. Stephens

1996
TEACHER IDEAS PRESS
A Division of
Libraries Unlimited, Inc.
Englewood, Colorado

We dedicate this book to
Wesley L. Stephens
for his steadfast interest in and support of our work.

TEACHER IDEAS PRESS
A Division of
Libraries Unlimited, Inc.
P.O. Box 6633
Englewood, CO 80155-6633
1-800-237-6124

Production Editor: Kevin W. Perizzolo
Design and Layout: Pamela J. Getchell

Library of Congress Cataloging-in-Publication Data

Brown, Jean E., 1945-
    Exploring diversity : literature themes and activities for grades
4-8 / Jean E. Brown, Elaine C. Stephens.
    x, 210 p. 22x28 cm.
    Includes bibliographical references and index.
    ISBN 1-56308-322-1
    1. Multiculturalism--Study and teaching (Elementary)
2. Multiculturalism--Study and teaching--Activity programs.
3. Pluralism (Social sciences) in literature.   4. Education,
Elementary--Activity programs.   I. Stephens, Elaine C., 1943-
II. Title.
    HM276.B76   1996
    305.8'0071'2--dc20
                                            95-47473
                                            CIP

Contents

Themes and Activities:
Getting Along with Others

Acknowledgments

We feel that literature is a gift that we have enjoyed and benefited from throughout our lives and our careers. We thank the many authors for those books that have had a lasting impact on us. We feel that a book like this is designed to help other teachers involve their students to experience the joy and power of literature.

This book is the result of the many years we have spent as teachers, both K-12 and college. We are grateful to the many students who have enriched our classrooms and our lives. This book is also an outgrowth of their love and commitment to literature. We especially thank our colleague and former student, Nadine Burke for her review of the manuscript and her insightful comments. We also thank Dallas Fischer and Hiroko Omukai for their contributions in so many different ways.

The team at Teacher Ideas Press has been unfailingly helpful. We thank Susan Zernial and Pamela J. Getchell for their help throughout this process. It is Kevin W. Perizzolo to whom we are especially grateful for assuming a project "in midstream" and facilitating its completion with humor, style, and professionalism.

Introduction

This book is designed to help teachers develop various ways of exploring diversity through incorporating multicultural literature into their curriculum. Throughout this book, we describe books and authors that give us insights and understanding about the diversity of our schools, our communities, our society, our nation, and our world. We also present a multitude of activities and suggestions for providing meaningful student interaction with this literature.

The chapters are as follows:

Ch 1: Teaching About Diversity Through Literature

Ch 2: Implementing Multicultural Literature

Ch 3: Heritage: Understanding Our Past

Ch 4: Identity: Seeking a Sense of Self

Ch 5: Identity: A Sense of Belonging

Ch 6: Getting Along with Others: Family

Ch 7: Getting Along with Others: Friends

Ch 8: Celebrating Diversity: Books and Authors Too Good to Miss

The contents of the book at a glance are: Chapter 1 presents a rationale for using multicultural literature in the classroom. Chapter 2 provides instructional models for using this literature. The models are the reader involvement model and implementation model.

Chapter 3 begins a series of five chapters that use themes and activities to heighten student involvement with the reading of multicultural literature. Chapter 3 helps students to explore racial, ethnic, and cultural traditions and heritage through the use of both contemporary realistic fiction and historical fiction.

Chapters 4 and 5 share the theme of identity. In Chapter 4 the focus is on developing a sense of self; whereas, in Chapter 5, the focus is on developing a sense of belonging or a sense of place.

Chapters 6 and 7 help students to examine the most significant relationships that young people have: relationships with members of their families and relationships with friends and peers.

Chapter 8 presents outstanding books that contribute to enhancing the perspective of diversity and award-winning authors who are recognized as contributing to cultural understanding with their works. It also provides a brief discussion of several major awards and their recipients.

This book is designed to be descriptive rather than prescriptive. We do not advocate any one single approach to teaching any book. We do provide teachers with options and springboards from which they can proceed in any direction that they believe to be appropriate. For example, in each of the themes and activities chapters, Chapters 3-7, we present a number of ways to help students experience a book through a thematic view or by using one or more of the activities presented. Additionally, many of the books are listed in more than one chapter because of their broadly conceptualized plots and multifaceted characterizations. We also are inclusive in our definition of multicultural literature. We include works that span several cultures as well as those that represent the major cultural group of the United States, those of European American descendants. In all cases, our single most important criterion is quality literature that promotes an understanding and acceptance of all cultures.

1

Teaching About Diversity Through Literature

When somebody can look at you and insult you because you're old, or because you're young, or because you're black, or because you're . . . you're whatever you are, it's all the same. And what it's not is funny!

Myers, Walter Dean. *Won't Know Till I Get There.* (1982, p. 148)

We strive to be a nation that looks at individuals and make judgments about them as individuals, not as members of particular groups. As educators, one of our primary goals is to help young people develop a sense of respect for themselves and for others. We do this, in part, by identifying those commonalties that all people share as well as by exploring and learning to value differences. These complex understandings are fostered when we provide young people with opportunities to learn about their own heritages and those of others through reading multicultural literature. Through this literature, youthful readers share the experiences of other young people, their dreams, their struggles, their victories, and their losses. From these vicarious experiences, young people can learn the important lesson that no matter how unique our heritages, there is more that unites us than separates us.

In this chapter, we examine how quality literature, in general, and multicultural literature, specifically, contributes to the development of young people. We also describe the characteristics of readers in grades four through eight and relate these to themes for exploring diversity through literature.

Authentic Connections with Literature

Quality literature has a powerful effect on readers. This power is there for classroom teachers to use as they strive to help young people become literate, learn about their world, and make personal connections with the curriculum. We believe that there is no other area in the curriculum that has the potential to elicit such significant responses from students as does literature. This belief is reaffirmed in Suzanne Fisher Staples' novel *Haveli* (1993, p.126). In this book, a sequel to *Shabanu,* Shabanu and her daughter are being tutored, and their teacher tells them:

> "I am taking you to a wonderful new world," said the widow, whose name was Samiya, standing before them for the first time. "Once you've learned to read, adventures you've never even imagined will unfold. You'll visit places you never knew existed. There will be no secret you cannot unlock."

This intense connection between the reader and the printed page has the ability to change readers as they are transported into the world of the book. When the reader and the book merge, an authentic connection is made, resulting in increased knowledge, deeper understandings, or new insights. Perhaps the power of literature is most widely recognized for its ability to evoke strong feelings from readers. The plight of characters whose lives are totally removed from their own can make readers understanding and sympathetic. Through literature, readers may recognize that characters experience the same kinds of challenges or victories that they have. Those kinds of connections allow readers to establish a one-to-one experience with characters and empathize with them. Aleksandr Solzhenitsyn, in his 1972 Nobel Acceptance Speech, discusses that type of connection as an affirmation of the inherent value of literature:

> "... [it] can overcome man's unfortunate trait of learning only through his own experience...recreating in the flesh what another has experienced, and allowing it to be acquired as one's own."

Our role as teachers is to provide many and varied experiences for students to interact with significant books and to encourage them to read widely so that they may create for themselves these authentic connections. When we consider the powerful benefits of using literature in the classroom, those benefits become even more exciting as we explore the opportunities that literature provides to help students to look beyond and understand more than their lives. Linda Hart-Hewins and Jan Wells (1992, p. 17) in their work with language arts programs for grades four through nine remind us that:

> Books are not to be prescribed like medicine to make students better people, or even to improve their reading skills . . .; they are encounters with ideas that somehow leave readers transformed. A good book should leave us thinking or feeling differently than we did before we read it.

Multicultural Literature in the Classroom

Multicultural literature is an effective avenue to help young people understand themselves, recognize their heritage, and acknowledge and value the cultures of others. The literature taught in our schools needs to reflect the diverse nature of American society. Students need to and have a right to read about people who share their cultural heritage. Author Nicholasa Mohr (1990, p. 79) describes her experiences:

> Growing up, I had never seen or read *any* book that included Puerto Ricans (or Hispanics, for that matter) as citizens who worked hard and contributed to this nation. In American letters, we were *invisible*.

Eleanora Tate in her novel, *The Secret of Gumbo Grove,* addresses the issue of young people needing to know about themselves and their heritage. The main character of her book, Raisin Stackhouse, loves history and wants to know why they never read about any black people when they study local history. She undertakes a project cleaning up the old church cemetery and discovers a great deal about the past that she shares with her community. Like Raisin, all young people should have opportunities to read about others like themselves.

Understanding one's heritage is only one facet of the benefits of using multicultural literature in the classroom. Students also gain an understanding and appreciation of the diverse groups within our pluralistic society. Cross-cultural understanding can help to eliminate confusion about and mistrust of anything that is different. When cultural differences remain hidden or misunderstood, fear and suspicion frequently overcome rational understanding. Learning about the customs, beliefs, and traditions of others helps students become more open to differences. This openness, when nurtured and developed, fosters tolerance. As a Hispanic student in Doris Walker-Dalhouse's (1992, p. 421) fifth grade class stated, "People need to know more, because some people treat us like we are not regular people."

Tolerance is a goal for all people because we can no longer assume that our lives will not be affected by the actions and policies of people across the world. We live in a global village; students cannot afford narrow, monolithic perspectives of the world, especially as they enter the twenty-first century. Doris Walker-Dalhouse (1992, p. 416) describes how she used African American literature to increase ethnic understanding in her fifth grade classroom whose composition was predominately students of Norwegian origin. She cites research that incorporating multiethnic literature into the curriculum expands students' awareness and decreases negative stereotyping of individuals from other cultures.

Crawford (1993, p. 25) identifies four contributions that multicultural literature makes to the classroom:

1. it provides students from diverse populations with reading materials, characters, themes, and plots that are more closely related to their life experiences.

2. it provides students with reading materials that challenge misconceptions and stereotypes and develop awareness and understanding of other cultures.

3. it gives students from diverse cultures positive role models who have overcome problems dealing with life and society. Story role models assist culturally diverse students in developing better self-concepts; they provide dominant-culture students with images of people from diverse cultures that assist in overcoming stereotypical biases.

4. it assists students to "walk in the shoes" of book characters from another culture to begin the process of gaining a new perspective.

The benefits of using multicultural literature become even more significant when we examine current conditions in our nation. Literature and the understandings that can be nurtured by reading about people from different cultures are significant tools in confronting persistent social problems: bias crimes and bigotry. During the last ten years we have witnessed an increase in the number of hate groups who target members of ethnic groups or other minorities. Their attacks often go beyond name-calling; they have destroyed property and even assaulted and murdered people for their ethnicity or beliefs. Education is the best weapon against violent acts. Using multicultural literature will provide younger readers with insights and ideas so that they can make thoughtful choices and take responsible actions. Kathryn H. Au (1993, p. 189) speaks to the value of multicultural literature for fostering a democratic society:

> In discussions of multiethnic literature, teachers guide students not only to interpret the text but also to reflect upon the ways that they might carry democratic values forward in their own lives. Teachers with a commitment to the values of democracy and diversity accept the challenge of using new patterns of literacy instruction to help the students who are in their classrooms today. Through their positive actions and those of their students, they also work toward a future when the United States will be a more just and fully democratic society, offering all children a wealth of educational opportunities.

Characteristics of Readers, Grades Four Through Eight

Young people in grades four through eight are eager to learn about the world. They are intensely curious and generally receptive to exploring new things. They undergo significant changes during these years, physically, emotionally, and intellectually. Accompanying these changes is an increased need to create their identities and define who they are and where they fit in with family, friends, and society at large. They feel tremendous pressure to belong and to find approval with their peers. They are concerned with questions of right and wrong and may become deeply interested in social and political issues.

Most students in grades four through eight are beyond the initial stages of literacy acquisition and are able to use reading and writing to learn new information and for personal enjoyment. They are able to make ever-increasingly sophisticated connections between their experiences and what they are reading. Still there is great variation among young people of this age. Many upper elementary school students become avid readers who "get lost in a book," while some still need lots of "easier" books to help them develop their reading potential. Numerous studies (Gallo, 1984; Bintz, 1993) indicate that after elementary school, however, many students' reading abilities no longer continue to grow and their interest in reading seems to decline during middle school and high school, especially their interest in school reading assignments. At this age students need to see "real" reasons for reading and writing and make authentic connections with what is important to them.

The themes described in this resource guide reflect some of the important needs and interests of young people, grades four through eight: identity, relationships, and heritage. These themes are explored in a variety of ways, by a variety of characters, and in a variety of settings in the books we recommend. As author Sandy Asher (1992, p. 79) states:

> Generally, adults choose books that reflect and reinforce attitudes they already hold. Young adult readers, on the other hand, are actively searching for ideas, information, and values to incorporate into their personalities and into their lives. The books they read become a very real part of them.

References

Asher, Sandy. 1992. "What about now? What about here? What about me?" In *Reading Their World*, edited by V. R. Monseau and G. M. Salvern. Portsmouth, NH: Heinemann.

Au, Kathryn H. 1993. *Literacy Instruction in Multicultural Settings*. Fort Worth, TX: Harcourt Brace Jovanovich.

Bintz, W. P. 1993. "Resistant readers in secondary education: Some insights and implications." *Journal of Reading* 36 (8). Newark, DE: International Reading Association.

Crawford, Leslie W. 1993. *Language and Literacy: Learning in Multicultural Classrooms*. Boston, MA: Allyn & Bacon.

Gallo, D. R. 1984. "Reactions to required reading: Some implications from a study of Connecticut students." *Connecticut English Journal* 15 (2).

Hart-Hewins, Linda and Jan Wells. 1992. *Read It in the Classroom! Organizing an Interactive Language Arts Program, Grades 4-9*. Portsmouth, NH: Heinemann.

Mohr, Nicholasa. 1990. "Nicholasa Mohr." In *Speaking for Ourselves*, edited by D. R. Gallo. Urbana, IL: National Council of Teachers of English.

Myers, Walter Dean. 1982. *Won't Know Till I Get There*. New York, NY: Scholastic.

Solzhenitsyn, Aleksandr. 1972. *Nobel Lecture*. New York, NY: Farrar, Straus and Giroux.

Staples, Suzanne Fisher. 1993. *Haveli*. New York, NY: Alfred A. Knopf.

Tate, Eleanora. 1987. *The Secret of Gumbo Grove*. New York, NY: Franklin Watts, Inc.

Walker-Dalhouse, Doris. February 1991. "Using African-American literature to increase ethnic understanding." *The Reading Teacher*, 45 (6). Newark, DE: International Reading Association.

2

Implementing Multicultural Literature

No area of the curriculum lends itself more readily to a multicultural approach than the teaching of literature.

ASCD Curriculum Update (September 1993, p. 4)

Reading multicultural literature provides students with two facets of learning about diversity. First, students have opportunities to discover and explore their heritages, cultures, and traditions. Second, they have opportunities to gain insights and perceptions about other cultures. These two facets complement and reinforce one another. As young people learn to value and respect themselves and their ethnic and cultural heritage, they have a basis for valuing and respecting others. This sense of connectedness is an important support for young people as they sort out who they are.

Teachers must be sensitive, however, to the need of young people to feel as if they "fit in." Students need to feel that they have a sense of control over what they do. A student should not be singled out and assigned a book for the sole reason that it matches the person's cultural or ethnic heritage. Neither should a student be forced to read about a different culture simply because it is different. Choice is crucial to the success of a multicultural literature program. Tolerance and understanding evolve through positive experiences, not through mandates. Some minority students are more comfortable reading initially about the dominant culture; others connect immediately with books that reflect their culture. Moreover, some students from the dominant culture may respond initially with disdain to stories reflecting experiences different from theirs, especially if they have no choice in selecting what they read. The most powerful inducement to get young people to read a book is the recommendation of a friend, classmate, or valued adult. A wealth of quality literature and engaging activities helps teachers to cope with the complexities of these situations.

The process of implementing a multicultural literature program in upper elementary and middle school classrooms is similar to planning and organizing for any student-centered literature program. The key is recognizing that students should have a variety of experiences that will allow them to have choices in what they read and how they interact with literature. They also need a variety of opportunities to respond to their reading and to share their responses. In this chapter, we present information, models, and guides for implementing multicultural literature. We begin by describing the Reader Involvement Model (Brown and Stephens, 1995), which examines the processes that readers go through as they become involved in reading literature. Then we present an Implementation Model that describes how teachers can provide for varied patterns of classroom organization to foster student interaction with their reading. Accompanying this model are a number of guide sheets that may be duplicated for use in the classroom.

Reader Involvement Model

Our goal is to use multicultural literature to help students move beyond being readers of words to being readers of literature who recognize and appreciate its power to make a difference in their lives. Too often when students are assigned to read materials that they have no connection with, they simply go through the motions. The underlying premise of the Reader Involvement Model is that if students are to move beyond pronouncing words to constructing meaning, they must have literary experiences that evoke a commitment from them as readers. To connect with it, a book must make enough of an impression on the reader that he or she will have a reaction to it. We have all witnessed students who don't remember anything about the story that they have just completed reading. Additionally, students need opportunities to respond to their reading through discussions and especially through writing. Through these kinds of interactions, reading literature will make a difference in the lives of students.

The Reader Involvement Model (Brown and Stephens, 1995) (figure 2.1) is designed to provide teachers with a framework that describes the processes that readers go through as they become involved with reading literature. The first stage in this model is the initiating stage when readers make decisions about what, when, and how they will read. This stage is crucial as teachers guide students to choose appropriate selections and prepare themselves for their interactions with them. In each of the thematic chapters in this book, we provide teachers with specific suggestions for initiating activities. The second stage is that of connecting when readers make connections between their reading and themselves, those around them, or the world in general. Student Involvement Experiences keyed into specific focus books are presented in each thematic chapter to aid in facilitating this second stage. The third stage is that of internalizing when readers affirm the connections and internalize reactions, beliefs, and understandings about what they have read. Each thematic chapter contains Responding and Reflecting activities to facilitate internalizing.

These three stages reflect involvement between the readers and the text with sharing as the ongoing dimension of the Reader Involvement Model. Involvement is enhanced when readers have a context in which they reflect and react to the initiating, connecting, and internalizing by sharing with others. In the context of the classroom, involvement is enhanced when teachers are able to provide an environment in which readers are able to share their reading experiences through a variety of activities. The remainder of this chapter provides teachers with help in establishing just such an environment.

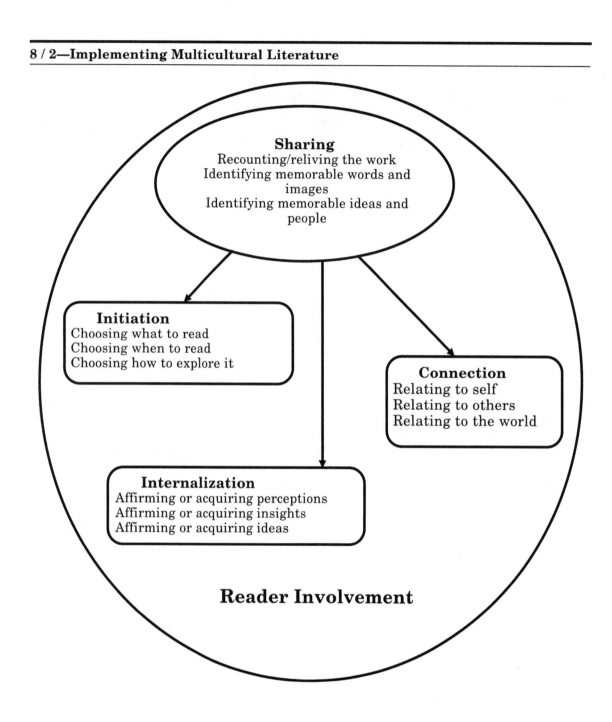

Fig. 2.1. Reader Involvement Model—(Brown and Stephens, 1995)

Implementation Model

For teachers who are seeking to incorporate multicultural literature into the curriculum, the initial question is "Where to begin?" There are a number of preliminary steps that teachers can take, but perhaps the most important one is simply to start reading multicultural literature for young people. There is no substitute for a teacher who is enthusiastic and knowledgeable about specific books and authors. Teachers can use any of the books recommended in this guide as a starting point. Additionally, the following suggestions will help teachers prepare for integrating multicultural literature into their programs:

1. Survey students to see the breadth of cultural heritage among them.

2. Review class materials to see how ethnicity is presented and addressed in literature anthologies, reading texts, social studies books, and other supplementary material.

3. Talk with the school librarian to learn what materials and services are available.

4. Visit the local public library (also visit any nearby college or university libraries).

5. Read books that are written on appropriate interest and reading levels for your students and begin matching them with your curriculum objectives.

6. Talk with colleagues to see how they are addressing multicultural literature in their classroom.

7. Collect professional books on the subject.

8. Contact genealogical libraries for information, guidelines for tracing one's heritage, and sample family tree charts.

9. Prepare a display of multicultural books for your classroom.

Once teachers have established a foundation for their integration of multicultural literature in their classrooms, they are ready to begin implementing it into the curriculum. Figure 2.2 presents teacher roles in implementation.

The Implementation Model describes three major roles for teachers: planning and organizing, instructing and facilitating, and responding and reflecting. The model is based on the assumption that students will be involved in a series of discoveries of self, connections, and heritage. To facilitate this type of learning, the classroom emphasis is on a variety of student experiences with literature. The teacher prepares for these experiences through several organizational approaches designed to stimulate and maintain student interest and positive involvement: whole class, small group or pairs with learning partners, and individual. Next the teacher provides direction for student experiences by deciding learning objectives, selecting teaching strategies that arouse curiosity, create interest, and promote involvement for all students, and providing support for students as they interact with the literature. Finally, the teacher engages in responding and reflecting by providing feedback to students. The thematic chapters in this book contain suggestions and activities to assist teachers in using the Implementation Model. Additionally, the following forms are designed to be copied and used to facilitate classroom organization. Directions for their use are as follows:

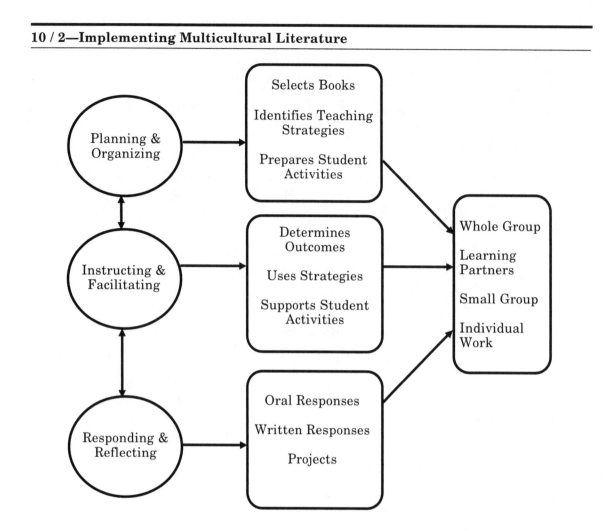

Figure 2.2. Implementation Model

Class Logs—a daily record of pertinent class information to aid students who are absent or who have difficulty understanding or remembering; responsibility for keeping class log rotates among students

Small Group Project Journal—record of group progress; responsibility of group recorder can rotate among group members

Small Group Project Evaluation Sheet—evaluation of group work using rating scale; each member completes sheet individually

Self-Evaluation for Individual Work—evaluation of contributions to group work using written responses; each member completes form

Individual Evaluations—evaluation of each group member using the rating scale; each member fills out the form for self and all other group members

Student Self-Assessment Form—information on individual reading interests; completed by each student

Student Reading Record Form—information related to a specific book; completed by each student

Class Logs

Course Title:
Date:
Announcements:

Class Notes:

Other Information:

Signed:

Small Group Project Journal

Date: _____   Recorder: _____

Members Present: _____

_____

_____

_____

_____

_____

_____

Planning Summary:

Individual Assignments:

Timeline/ Deadlines:

Small Group Project Evaluation Form

Respond on a scale of 1-5; 5 is the highest score

Name: _____

1. Our project fulfilled the assignment.   1 2 3 4 5

2. Our project was a cooperative endeavor.   1 2 3 4 5

3. We spent our work time productively.   1 2 3 4 5

4. Our project helped me to understand the topic better.   1 2 3 4 5

5. Our project helped other class members to understand the topic better.   1 2 3 4 5

6. All members of the group did their share.   1 2 3 4 5

Comments:

Self-Evaluation for Individual Work

Name: _____ Date: _____

Title of Project:

Personal Objectives for Project:

Did You Meet These Objectives? How?

What Book(s) Did You Read?

How Did You Rate Them?

What Did You Learn from This Project?

Comments and Reactions:

Individual Evaluations

Self-evaluation   Name _____

Positive participation	1 2 3 4 5
Completed assignments	1 2 3 4 5
Met deadlines	1 2 3 4 5
Quality of Contribution	1 2 3 4 5

Comments:

Group Member Evaluation   Name _____

Positive participation	1 2 3 4 5
Completed assignments	1 2 3 4 5
Met deadlines	1 2 3 4 5
Quality of Contribution	1 2 3 4 5

Comments:

Group Member Evaluation   Name _____

Positive participation	1 2 3 4 5
Completed assignments	1 2 3 4 5
Met deadlines	1 2 3 4 5
Quality of Contribution	1 2 3 4 5

Comments:

Group Member Evaluation   Name _____

Positive participation	1 2 3 4 5
Completed assignments	1 2 3 4 5
Met deadlines	1 2 3 4 5
Quality of Contribution	1 2 3 4 5

Comments:

Student Self-Assessment Form

The best book I ever read was _____

The best book I read in the last year was _____

The worst book I ever read was _____

The worst book I read in the last year was _____

My favorite kind of books to read are _____

	Always	Frequently	Sometimes	Never
I enjoy reading				
My favorite leisure time activity is reading				
I like to learn about my family's heritage				
The best way to learn is to read				

Student Reading Record Form

Name: _____   Date/Term _____

Book _____

Date Begun: _____   Date Finished: _____

Memorable Moments

Unforgettable Characters

Rating

References

Brown, Jean E. and Elaine C. Stephens. 1995. *Teaching Young Adult Literature: Sharing the Connection*. Belmont, CA: Wadsworth.

Choosing Multicultural Literature. September 1993. *ASCD Curriculum Update*. Alexandria, VA: Association for Supervision and Curriculum Development.

Themes and Activities

3

Heritage:
Understanding Our Past

As we explore themes that are recurring in multicultural young adult literature, the theme of exploring one's heritage as a means of understanding the past is an appropriate foundation. In all of the thematic chapters, we will be examining the significance of the connections in life. In this chapter, we will investigate a type of connection that is abstract and less direct in many people's lives than connections between people: the connection that exists between an individual and his or her cultural, racial, and ethnic heritage. It is this connection that reaffirms and supports the diversity in our society. For first and second generation Americans, their cultural traditions are frequently still a part of their experiences, but customs are often forgotten when they are not regularly observed. Furthermore, for many years people supported the belief that our society was a melting pot and all newcomers should abandon their language and customs to fit in here. For many immigrants who came here believing that in a new land the opportunities were limitless, fitting into the mainstream of American culture was of paramount importance. Many cultural and religious customs were abandoned and a sense of continuity with the past and an understanding of traditions were lost. In recent years the idea of ethnic pride and a valuing of the diverse nature of our society have emerged.

For young people who are beginning to gain a sense of their cultural heritage, it is important that they not be mislead to confuse cultural pride with ethnocentrism. Inherent in learning about one's heritage should be the recognition that all cultures have value. Cultural awareness and pride should promote cross-cultural understandings. The sense of security and pride that students develop as they study their heritage should help them to be more accepting of others and more tolerant of differences.

Goals

As you use this chapter with your students, the following goals will provide a focus in their exploration of the theme of understanding our past.

- An understanding of our heritage helps us to value ourselves and our traditions.

- A knowledge of the heritage of other people helps us to understand customs and traditions that differ from our own.

- An understanding of cultural and ethnic heritage helps us to value the contributions of everyone's ancestors to the United States.

- An understanding of cultural and ethnic heritage helps us to be more tolerant of differences.

- An understanding of cultural and ethnic heritage helps us to recognize the unfairness and dangers of prejudice and stereotypes.

Chapter Overview

The Reader Involvement Model, presented in Chapter 2, describes student experiences with the reading of literature. Central to that model is the idea of providing opportunities for students to share what they are reading with each other in a number of ways.

We have included a number of opportunities for students to share their reactions, thoughts, and feelings with one another through journals, role playing, creative projects, and discussions. Sharing their reactions, thoughts, and feelings is an on-going process for students as they read multicultural literature to explore diversity.

In this chapter, the theme of heritage: understanding our past will be explored in a number of ways. First, we examine a series of quotes from focus books (In Their Own Words) that are related to the theme. Following this are Initiating Experiences. This is designed to create reader interest in the theme. This process of initiating is the first stage of the Reader Involvement Model.

In the next section, Reading and Connecting Experiences, we explore the theme of heritage: understanding our past and focus on specific titles in which that theme is a significant part of the book. We begin with picture books, focusing on one specific picture book and recommending others. We then use fiction and nonfiction to examine the theme. The discussion of each individual book, picture book or novel, is followed by Responding Activities, an opportunity for student involvement. These activities, while focused on specific books, are designed to help students become involved with their reading by responding in ways that help them to feel connected to the work. This sense of connection represents the kind of response that occurs in the second stage of the Reader Involvement Model.

After students have read the book(s) on the theme, they need additional opportunities to interact more fully with the books so that they will internalize their understanding. The follow-up activities are entitled Reflecting and Internalizing. These help readers move on to other titles, building on their understanding and experiences with their reading. These processes correspond to the third stage of the response model. Cross-curricular connections are made in the section, Connections Across the Curriculum. Finally, the chapter concludes with a listing of other books, Further Reading.

In Their Own Words

Each of the themes that we discuss in this book is presented in various ways by the focus books. Presenting quotations related to the theme or from the literature your students will be reading is an excellent way to get students thinking and talking about the topic. The following examples relate to diversity and a sense of heritage, understanding our past.

In this book, we are using these quotes as a type of initiating experience; however, there are a number of other ways that quotes can be used to heighten student involvement with their reading. Among the other ways that quotes can be used in the classroom are as a preview by having students speculate about the theme before they read the book; or as a focusing tool as they are reading; or as a post-reading discussion or writing prompt.

> Give me your tired, your poor,
> Your huddled masses yearning to breathe free . . .
>
> Inscription on the Statue of Liberty

The very richness of American life lies in the fact that the United States is not a "melting pot" in which everyone has merged into a featureless, gray mass. Rather, it is a mosaic, made up of people from numerous cultures who take pride and pleasure in their origins. That, after all, is what our individual family stories are all about.

Perl, L. *The Great Ancestor Hunt.* 1989, p. 69.

For those of you who are immigrants, maybe parts of these stories will remind you of your own experiences. Maybe you will feel a little less alone realizing that what you're going through has been shared by others in the past and will be shared by even newer immigrants in the future.

For those born in the United States, maybe you'll gain a perspective on the global village that lies beyond your own tight circle of friends. Maybe you will come to understand that our nation is richer because it is a rainbow of cultures and different points of view.

Bode, J. *New Kids in Town, Oral Histories of Immigrant Teens.* 1989, p. 19.

"But—" Sundara had to smile. It was so obvious. "If I am the girl next door, I am not Sundara Sovann. I am not the girl he like. Cannot separate someone from their past. I am everything I already live through. Just as you are."

Crew, L. *Children of the River.* 1989, p. 161.

I felt sadder than ever, for when my mother told me we were leaving I hadn't realized everything we owned would have to stay behind and that all the familiar bits and pieces that went to make up our life would disappear. Everything we were leaving behind would grow small, but not so small that we would ever forget it.

Whelan, Gloria. *Goodbye, Vietnam.* 1992. p. 19, 135.

For all eternity she is doomed to walk by the banks of the river, searching for her children. On many a cold and dark night you can hear her crying and calling for her children. Her long, loud, mourning cry of grief often comes disguised as the sound of the wind by the river.

from "The Weeping Woman (La Llorona)," in *The Corn Woman: Stories and Legends of the Hispanic Southwest,* retold by Angel Vigil, 1994.

"Mom, I just want to find out about my background—my heritage—it doesn't have anything to do with how I feel about you and Dad."

Okimoto, J. D. *Molly by Any Other Name.* 1990, p. 99.

Initiating Experiences

The following suggestions are intended to use with students to initiate the theme study. They are designed to help students to relate to the theme, to make their prior knowledge active, and to arouse their interest in it. To help students become involved with their reading we suggest varied types of experiences, oral activities or discussions, and writing experiences. These activities are related to the initiating stage of the Reader Involvement Model.

- In your class, brainstorm what stereotypes are. Then identify what stereotypes are used for people with your cultural or ethnic heritage. How do these stereotypes make you feel? How do you respond to them?

- Select one of your ancestors or someone you know who immigrated to this country. Identify the year he or she arrived in the United States. Research that year to see what the conditions would have been for an immigrant.

- Create your own picture book about a family member, a family tradition, or a family outing by collecting photos or doing your own drawings and then adding appropriate captions.

Responding Activity: Viewing Discussion Guide

During the next week read the newspaper, watch television, and observe how people interact. Keep a log of situations where you observe stereotypes and uses of prejudicial language. Share and compare findings with your group.

	Stereotypes	Prejudicial Language
Newspapers		
Television		
Observation		

Response Log

Write about a custom that your family shares. Ask your parents and other relatives where the custom came from. Is it a tradition from your cultural heritage, or is it something unique that your family developed?

Response Log

Ask your parents and grandparents if your family has any heirlooms that represent your heritage. Describe them.

Exploring Diversity. © 1996. Teacher Ideas Press. (800) 237-6124.

Reading and Connecting Experiences

Picture Book

Picture books can be used effectively with older students to introduce them to a topic or to initiate class discussion. There are many excellent picture books that illustrate the diversity and richness of cultural, racial, and ethnic heritage.

Ancona, George. *Pablo Remembers, The Fiesta of the Day of the Dead*. Lothrop, Lee & Shepard Books, 1993.

Pablo and his family observe the three day festival of the dead, which is an opportunity to honor their ancestors. The text accompanied by photographs relates all of the traditional activities and customs that the people of Pablo's village in Mexico observe. The festival has a special meaning for Pablo because it is a time for him to feel close to his grandmother who died two years before.

When reading this picture book, help your students watch or listen for the use of Spanish words. Have them discuss what they mean and what they add to the book.

Responding Activities. See page 29.

OTHER PICTURE BOOKS

Ancona, George. *Pablo Remembers, The Fiesta of the Day of the Dead*.

Collier, John. *The Backyard*.

Garland, Sherry. Illustrated by Tatsuro Kiuchi. *The Lotus Seed*.

Hausman, Gerald. Illustrated by Cara Moser and Barry Moser. *Turtle Island ABC, A Gathering of Native American Symbols*.

Johnson, Dolores. *Now Let Me Fly, The Story of a Slave Family*.

Lyon, George Ella. Illustrated by Peter Catalanotto. *Who Came Down That Road?*

MacLachlan, Patricia. Pictures by Pertzoff. *Three Names*.

Musgrove, Margaret. Pictures by Leo Dillon and Diane Dillon. *Ashanti to Zulu, African Traditions*.

Polacco, Patricia. *The Keeping Quilt*.

Rylant, Cynthia. Illustrated by Barry Moser. *Appalachia, The Voices of Sleeping Birds*.

Say, Allen. *Grandfather's Journey*.

Williams, David. Illustrated by Wiktor Sadowski. *Grandma Essie's Covered Wagon*.

Winter, Jeanette. *Follow the Drinking Gourd*.

Yolen, Jane. Illustrated by David Shannon. *Encounter*.

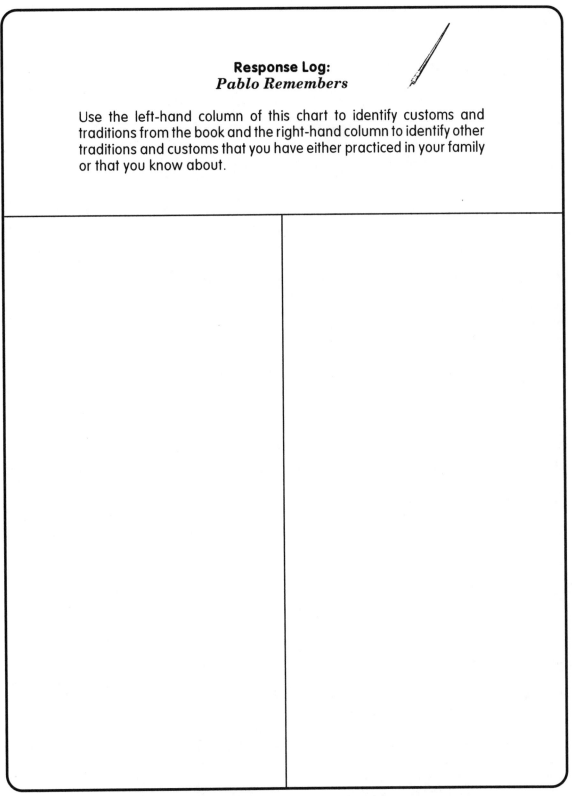

Response Log:
Pablo Remembers

Use the left-hand column of this chart to identify customs and traditions from the book and the right-hand column to identify other traditions and customs that you have either practiced in your family or that you know about.

Focus Books

Focus books for this chapter are those in which the theme, understanding our past and our heritage, is central to the book. These are books that have broad appeal and might be read and enjoyed by most students. We recommend that you select one or more of these titles for large group or whole class study.

Bode, Janet. *New Kids in Town, Oral Histories of Immigrant Teens.* Scholastic, 1989. 126 pages.

Freedman, Russell. *Immigrant Children.* Scholastic, 1980. 72 pages.

Perl, Lila. *The Great Ancestor Hunt.* Clarion Books, 1989. 104 pages.

Each of these books is a nonfiction work that deals with some aspects of the immigrant experience in the United States. Bode's work is a contemporary one in which she interviews teenagers who have recently immigrated to this country. These young people come from widely diverse backgrounds and countries. Freedman's work presents an historical perspective from the late 1800s through the first two decades of the 1900s. Most of the young people he describes were of European heritage. As is the trademark of his work, Freedman's text is complemented by wonderful and powerful photographs of young people of the time. These photos capture the difficulties the immigrants experienced. The last book of this group is Perl's *The Great Ancestor Hunt,* a guidebook for readers to start to discover their heritage. She provides interesting information about names and provides suggestions about how to find out about one's family heritage. It also includes some interesting photographs illustrating the past.

Students should understand that except for Native Americans, all of us are immigrants or descendants of immigrants. These books can begin to provide students with an awareness of part of the immigrant experience, both past and present. As they read the books, they can look for experiences that are similar to any of their family's or friends' experiences. *The Great Ancestor Hunt, The Fun of Finding Out Who You Are* is an excellent resource book that can used to generate many fascinating projects. Other books that will interest your students are the *Tracing Our Roots* books from The American Origins Series published by John Muir Publications.

Responding Activities. See page 34.

Hansen, Joyce. *Which Way Freedom?* Avon, 1986. 120 pages.

———. *Out from This Place.* Avon, 1988. 135 pages.

These two books provide insights into the Civil War and early Reconstruction period from the perspectives of two former slaves. The first book is from the point of view of a young Black man, Obie, who escapes with Easter from the plantation where they were slaves. Obie, Easter, and a young boy named Jason are the only family that any of them has. Initially, they are captured by the Confederates and must work for the Army, but when the Union forces attack, Obie escapes again. This time he ends up with the Union forces, but initially he still is not free. He works for the Union until the Emancipation Proclamation when he can join the Union forces to fight for the North. Whereas the first book focuses on Obie, the second book focuses on Easter. She is distressed that they had to leave Jason behind when they escaped. She is determined to return to get the boy. She disguises herself as a boy to work for the

Confederates and later returns "home" to look for Jason when she can get away from the Confederates. She gets to the plantation in time to rescue Jason and leave with another group of runaways heading for the Union lines. Once their group reaches the Yankee lines, Easter then has a new goal—for them to be united with Obie. While working for the Union, Easter prepares herself for a life of freedom after the war, but she never gives up hope that they will be together with Obie.

The setting for these two books is the South during the Civil War and the period immediately following it, the Reconstruction. Before reading these books, activate or develop your students' prior knowledge about life during this time to enhance their understanding of the plots and characters. You may want to follow up these books with Joyce Hansen's nonfiction book, *Between 2 Fires, Black Soldiers in the Civil War.*

Easter is a strong female character who captures the imagination of many young people. Have your students focus on how Easter grows and develops throughout these two books. Since Easter is a young person with strong values, you may also want your students to identify her values, the conflicts that she experiences as a result of them, and how she resolves these conflicts.

Responding Activities. Character mapping (Brown and Stephens, 1995, p. 244-45) is a useful tool to understand the process of characterization in literature. In this process, put the name of the character in a box in the middle of your paper. Then identify characteristics and qualities of that character and list each one individually in circles around the original box. Attach these new circles to each characteristic with lines leading back to the original circle.

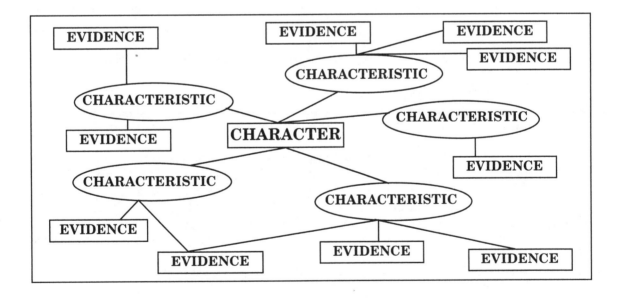

Next, find support or evidence for the characteristics from the reading. The evidence or support is placed in other shapes around the appropriate characteristic with lines going back to it. Remember that the evidence may be found in a number of ways: the character's speech, actions, and behaviors; other character's descriptions or comments; events; commentary from the narrator; illustrations; or the evidence may be inferred rather than directly stated. The evidence may also demonstrate more than one characteristic; therefore, it may have more than one line leading to more than one characteristic.

Levitin, Sonia. *Journey to America*. Scholastic, 1970. 150 pages.

It is 1938 and Lisa Platt and her family are increasingly worried by Nazi treatment of Jews in Germany. Some family members and friends urge them to leave, while others think they should stay. Papa goes to America to secure work and the immigration papers that will allow Lisa, her two sisters, and mother to come, also. Meanwhile, they flee to Switzerland, telling Nazi officials they are going for a short vacation. Unable to take goods or very much money with them, they encounter numerous hardships as they await word from Papa that he has permission for them to go to America, too. Lisa is befriended by a Catholic family that helps her and her family. Finally, they are granted permission to go to America.

The setting for this book is Germany and Switzerland on the eve of the Second World War. Before reading this book, activate or develop your students' prior knowledge about Nazism and the treatment of Jews to enhance their understanding of the story. There are many other powerful books, both fiction and nonfiction, written about this period that you may want to make available as a follow-up for your students.

This book provides young people with opportunities to explore the difficult choices and hardships that families must sometimes face. Friendships are also an important aspect of the story. Additionally, this book demonstrates how people may have different religious beliefs, but still help each other in times of need.

Responding Activities. See page 35.

Speare, Elizabeth George. *The Sign of the Beaver*. Dell, 1983. 135 pages.

Twelve-year-old Matt is left at the homestead he and his father built in the Maine wilderness while his father returns to Boston to bring the rest of the family to their new home. Matt is to keep the garden going and prepare provisions for the winter ahead when the family will be reunited. When Matt runs into trouble with an angry swarm of bees, he is helped by two Indians, Saknis and his grandson, Attean. Matt and Attean become friends and they teach one another many things. In the absence of Matt's family, Attean's family is helpful and supportive of him.

Before reading this book, activate or develop your students' prior knowledge about living conditions in the 1700s. Students also need to have an understanding of the effect of the settlers on the Native Americans. It will enhance their enjoyment of the story if they are aware of the vast difference between daily life then and now. Help them to understand that it was not unusual for youngsters Matt's age to assume adult responsibilities to help the family survive.

Responding Activities. See page 36.

Vigil, Angel. Translated by Jennifer Audrey Lowell and Juan Francisco Marín. *The Corn Woman: Stories and Legends of the Hispanic Southwest*. Libraries Unlimited, Inc., 1994. 234 pages.

This collection of tales and folklore of the Hispanic southwest is designed to capture the stories of the heritage of those who have settled in that area. The book is divided into four parts. The first includes a historical perspective of the Aztec culture and its evolution with the Spanish arrival. The merger of the Indio-Hispano cultures provided the basis for the stories that were brought to the southwest. The second part, the major section of the book, includes a thematic collection of traditional stories that represent the major cultural conventions. The third part relates stories of contemporary writers. The final part includes a glossary, bibliography, and information about the contributors. The book also contains photographs of art work in color.

This book provides an excellent background about folklore, the oral tradition, and the traditions of the southwest. Helping students to understand both the genre and the culture before reading the book will enhance their understanding of it.

Responding Activities. See page 37.

Yep, Laurence. *Dragon's Gate*. HarperCollins, 1993. 275 pages.

During the Civil War, the importance of the railroad became obvious, so at the war's end, the decision to span the nation with a railroad seemed sensible. The work was very difficult so American businessmen hired immigrant laborers to lay the tracks to connect east with west. The rugged mountains of the western United States presented special challenges. It was here that Otter, a young Chinese boy, ended up when he was forced to flee China. He had dreams of the riches and opportunities in America, but the reality did not match his dreams. The working conditions were brutal and he had to struggle just to survive.

The setting for this book is China and the western United States during the last half of the nineteenth century. Before reading it, activate or develop your students' prior knowledge about this time period in our history to enhance their understanding of the story. While reading it, you can help to foster your students' understanding of geography by finding locations on the map described in the book.

The character of Otter is central to this story. Students can trace the changes in Otter as he grows and develops. His changing relationship with his father is also significant. This story provides excellent opportunities to help students understand imagery and symbolism.

Responding Activities. See page 38.

Responding Activity:
Family Genealogy

Begin developing a family tree (see the following format). Each entry should include the person's name and date and place of birth if you can find them.

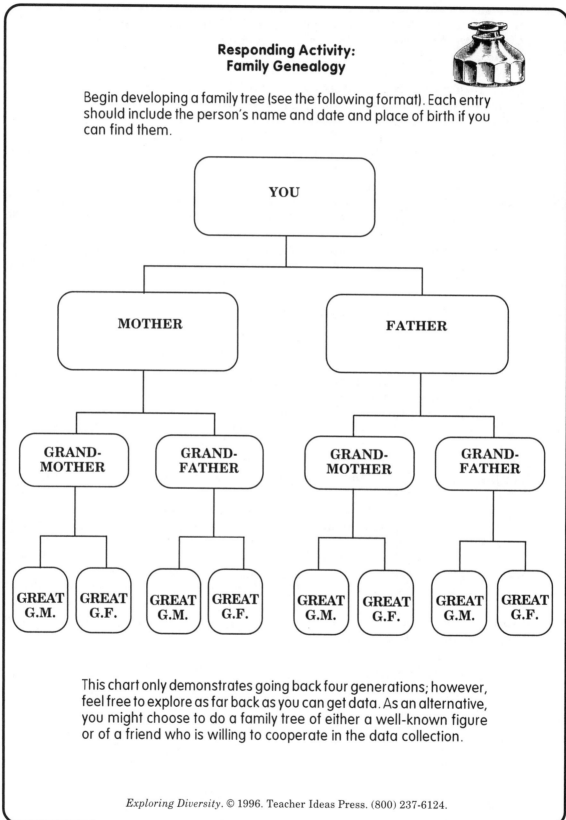

This chart only demonstrates going back four generations; however, feel free to explore as far back as you can get data. As an alternative, you might choose to do a family tree of either a well-known figure or of a friend who is willing to cooperate in the data collection.

Response Log:
Journey to America

Imagine that you and your family had to flee from the United States.
Draw a map tracing the route you would take. What might you see?
How would you get help?

Response Log:
The Sign of the Beaver

As you read the book, compile a list of customs, practices, and beliefs that were similar and different between Attean's people and the white settlers.

Response Log:
The Corn Woman

Write a story about your family as a legend or folktale.

Response Log:
Dragon's Gate

Keep track of the number of references that Yep makes to dragons. What significance do dragons have to the story?

Reflecting and Internalizing Experiences

In this section, we have selected activities to help students respond to and reflect upon books that they have read. The activities are designed to be general enough so that they can be applied to a number of different books rather than used with only a specific one. These activities can also be modified and adapted to be applied to specific books.

Use the following suggestions with students to aid them in responding to the books they are reading or to help students to reflect upon the theme and to extend their understanding of it. These experiences are varied, including oral activities or discussions, either small group or whole class; writing experiences in Reflection Logs; and exploration or creative activities, either small group or individual. These activities are designed to help students to internalize their reading and are related to the internalizing stage of the Reader Involvement Model. While some of the activities may include more than one of these types, each will be categorized according to the emphasis of student activity.

- Based on your reading, develop a script for a family who is having trouble entering this country through Ellis Island. Along with your classmates, perform it for the class.

- Develop a script dramatizing a scene from the book you have read. Along with some of your classmates, perform it for the class.

- Act out one of the scenes from Turner's *Take a Walk in Their Shoes.*

- Role play saying goodbye to your best friend when you and your family must emigrate to another country. Explain why you must leave and what your hopes and fears are.

- Develop a conversation between characters from two books who are of the same ethnic origin or from the same country.

- There are several organizations that may have information about your ancestors. Write to find out what they provide and how to do research. Among them are:

  Immigration and Naturalization Service
  10th St. and Constitution Ave. N.W.
  Washington, D.C. 20530

  Genealogical Society of Utah
  50 East North Temple St.
  Salt Lake City, Utah 84150

  Afro-American Historical and Genealogical Society
  Box 022340
  Brooklyn, New York 11202-0049

- Try to find out if any of your relatives entered this country through Ellis Island. Write a description of their experiences.

- Write a letter to yourself to be opened when you graduate from high school. Date it and describe your daily life as well as current events, popular songs, films, and famous people. Give it to your parents to keep, or if it is a class project, to your teacher.

- Talk to your family members about how you were named. Do any of your names have a special significance?

- Imagine that you must leave your native land to emigrate to another country. How would you feel? What five things would you take with you to help you remember home?

- Research your family's surname to see if you can determine its origin. There are books that can help you such as *The Mountain of Names: A History of the Human Family* by Alex Shoumatoff (Simon and Schuster Publishers, 1985).

- Create a picture book patterned after Lyon's *Who Came Down That Road?* Base it on your own heritage.

- Create an alphabet book based on your cultural or ethnic heritage or that of one that interests you.

- Create a picture book that tells the story of your ancestors.

- Write a short story based on the experiences of your ancestors.

- Design a mural that shows the history of your own ancestors or of those from books you have reading.

- Using the song in Winter's *Follow the Drinking Gourd* as a springboard or, based on one of the books you have read, compose a song about your ancestors.

- Using some of the folk literature as a springboard, write a myth or legend.

- After reading Coerr's *Sadako,* find out more about Sadako Sasaki, Folded Crane Clubs, and Peace Day.

- Use the book *L'ong Is a Dragon, Chinese Writing for Children* by Peggy Goldstein (Scholastic, 1991) to help you learn to write some Chinese characters.

CONNECTIONS ACROSS THE CURRICULUM

Students can increase their depth and breadth of understanding when they have opportunities to make connections among various content areas. The following suggestions are designed to help students relate this theme across the curriculum.

Art

- Study the art of a set period from the country of origin of some of your family. What characteristics do you think are typical?

Social Studies

- Research the country of origin of some of your family members. Especially try to discover what the social, political, and economic conditions were when your family left.

- Do research on immigration policies in this country. How have they changed over the years? Where did most immigrants come from in 1850, 1875, 1900, 1925, 1950, 1975, and 1990?

- Make a list of the items you would put in a time capsule to be opened 100 years from now. Explain why you selected each item.

Science

- Identify scientists from the country of origin of some of your family members.

- Select one scientific breakthrough that has come from that country and write a report about it.

Math

- Using the data you collected on immigration, graph the trends that you see. Be sure to write a legend explaining your chart.

- Then write three story problems for other students to solve with data from the immigration graph you developed.

- Find a picture of the Statue of Liberty. Estimate its dimensions. Then research the actual dimensions.

Geography

- Make a poster tracing your family's history beginning with the earliest ancestor that you can find out about and show where he or she came from.

Music

- What kind of music is composed and played in the country of origin of some of your family members? Research what contributions the people of that country have made to the field of music.

Physical Education and Sports

- Find out what kind of sports are played in a country of your family origin. Do they have professional teams? What kinds of games do young people play?

Further Reading

These titles relate to the theme of this chapter and could be used for whole class, small group, or individual reading.

Folk Literature from Many Cultures

Aardema, Verna. *Borreguita and the Coyote: Tale from Ayutha, Mexico.*

Alexander, Lloyd. Illustrated by Trina Schart Hyman. *The Fortune-Tellers.*

Bruchac, Joseph, and Jonathan London. Illustrated by Thomas Locker. *Thirteen Moons on Turtle's Back, A Native American Year of Moons.*

Climo, Shirley. Illustrated by Ruth Heller. *The Egyptian Cinderella.*

Coerr, Eleanor. Illustrated by Ed Young. *Sadako.*

Cohen, Caron Lee, retold by. Illustrated by Shonto Begay. *The Mud Pony.*

Cohlene, Terri, written and adapted by. Illustrated by Charles Reasoner. *Little Firefly, An Algonquian Legend.*

Cohlene, Terri. Illustrated by Charles Reasoner. *Quillworker, A Cheyenne Legend.*

Esbensen, Barbara Juster. Illustrated by Helen K. Davie. *The Star Maiden.*

Hamilton, Virginia. Illustrated by Jerry Pinkney. *Drylongso.*

———. *In the Beginning: Creation Stories from Around the World.*

———, retold by. Illustrated by Leo Dillon and Diane Dillon. *The People Could Fly, American Black Folktales.*

Hayes, Joe. *The Day It Snowed Tortillas: Tales from Spanish New Mexico.*

———. *La Llorona: The Weeping Woman.*

Joseph, Lynn. *The Mermaid's Twin Sister: More Stories from Trinidad.*

Lawson, Julie, retold by. Paintings by Paul Morin. *The Dragon's Pearl.*

Malotki, Ekkehart, retold by. Illustrated by Michael Lacapa. *The Mouse Couple, A Hopi Folktale.*

McDermott, Gerald, adapted and illustrated by. *Arrow to the Sun, A Pueblo Indian Tale.*

McKissack, Patricia. *The Dark-Thirty, Southern Tales of the Supernatural.*

Rhoads, Dorothy. *The Corn Grows Ripe.*

Sis, Peter. *A Small Tall Tale from the Far Far North.*

Vuong, Lynette Dyer. *The Brocaded Slipper and Other Vietnamese Tales.*

Yep, Laurence. *The Rainbow People.*

Young, Richard, and Judy Dockrey Young, collected and edited by. *African-American Folktales for Young Readers.*

Across Cultures

Fox, Paula. *The Slave Dancer.*

Johnston, Johanna. *They Led the Way, 14 American Women.*

Keehn, Sally M. *I Am Regina.*

Levine, Ellen. *. . . If Your Name Was Changed at Ellis Island.*

Murphy, Jim. *Crossing America on an Immigrant Train.*

Sandler, Martin W. *Pioneers, A Library of Congress Book.*

Stein, R. Conrad. *The Bill of Rights.*

African American

Collier, James Lincoln, and Christopher Collier. *Jump Ship to Freedom.*

———. *War Comes to Willy Freeman.*

———. *Who Is Carrie?*

Freedman, Florence. *Two Tickets to Freedom: The True Story of William and Ellen Craft, Fugitive Slaves.*

Hamilton, Virginia. *Anthony Burns: The Defeat and Triumph of a Fugitive Slave.*

———. *The House of Dies Drear.*

Hansen, Joyce. *Between 2 Fires: Black Soldiers in the Civil War.*

———. *The Captive.*

Haskins, Jim. *One More River to Cross, The Stories of Twelve Black Americans.*

———. *Outward Dreams, Black Inventors and Their Inventions.*

Levine, Ellen. *Freedom's Children, Young Civil Rights Activists Tell Their Own Stories.*

Lyons, Mary E. *Letters from a Slave Girl, The Story of Harriet Jacobs.*

McCurdy, Michael, edited and illustrated by. *Escape from Slavery, The Boyhood of Frederick Douglass in His Own Words.*

Meltzer, Milton. *Mary McLeod Bethune, Voice of Black Hope.*

Moore, Eva. *The Story of George Washington Carver.*

Myers, Walter Dean. *Now Is Your Time! The African-American Struggle for Freedom.*

Paulsen, Gary. *NIGHTJOHN.*

Petry, Ann. *Tituba of Salem Village.*

Rappaport, Doreen. *Escape from Slavery, Five Journeys to Freedom.*

Rupert, Janet. *The African Mask.*

Siegel, Beatrice. *The Year They Walked.*

Sterling, Dorothy. *Freedom Train, The Story of Harriet Tubman.*

Stein, R. Conrad. *The Montgomery Bus Boycott.*

Tate, Eleanora E. *The Secret of Gumbo Grove.*

———. *Thank You, Dr. Martin Luther King, Jr.!*

Turner, Glennette Tilley. *Take a Walk in Their Shoes.*

Walker, Mildren Pitts. *Mississippi Challenge.*

Yates, Elizabeth. *Amos Fortune, Free Man.*

Asia

Choi, Sook Nyul. *Echoes of the White Giraffe.*

———. *Year of Impossible Goodbyes.*

Nhuong, Huynh Quang. *The Land I Lost, Adventures of a Boy in Vietnam.*

Whelan, Gloria. *Goodbye, Vietnam.*

Asian American

Crew, Linda. *Children of the River.*

Houston, Jeanne Wakatsuki, and James D. Houston. *Farewell to Manzanar.*

Hoyt-Goldsmith, Diane. Photographs by Lawrence Migdale. *Hoang Anh, A Vietnamese-American Boy.*

Okimoto, Jean Davies. *Molly by Any Other Name.*

Uchida, Yoshiko. *Journey Home.*

———. *A Jar of Dreams.*

Yep, Laurence. *Child of the Owl.*

Caribbean Islands

O'Dell, Scott. *My Name Is Not Angelica.*

Central America

Castaneda, Omar S. *Among the Volcanoes.*

European American

Blos, Joan W. *A Gathering of Days.*

Duffy, James. *Radical Red.*

Moscinski, Sharon. *Tracing Our Irish Roots.*

European Immigrant

Angell, Judie. *One Way to Ansonia.*

Colman, Hila. *Rachel's Legacy.*

Gross, Virginia T. *It's Only Goodbye, An Immigrant Story.*

Nixon, Joan Lowery. *A Family Apart.*

———. *A Place to Belong.*

———. *Land of Dreams.*

———. *Land of Hope.*

———. *Land of Promise.*

Stein, R. Conrad. *Ellis Island.*

Holocaust

Adler, David A. *We Remember the Holocaust.*

Matas, Carol. *Daniel's Story.*

Reiss, Johanna. *The Upstairs Room.*

Siegal, Aranka. *Upon the Head of a Goat.*

Inuit

Rogers, Jean. *Goodbye, My Island.*

Jewish

Lasky, Kathy. *The Night Journey.*

Sagan, Miriam. *Tracing Our Jewish Roots.*

Mexico

Behrens, June. *Fiesta: Cinco de Mayo.*

Clendenen, Mary Jo. *Gonzalo: Coronado's Shepherd Boy.*

Mexican American

Bruin, Mary Ann. *Rosita's Christmas Wish.*

Native American

Bennett, James. *Dakota Dream.*

Blos, Joan W. *Brothers of the Heart.*

Hobbs, Will. *Beardance.*

Hudson, Jan. *Sweetgrass.*

O'Dell, Scott. *Island of the Blue Dolphins.*

———. *Sing Down the Moon.*

O'Dell, Scott, and Elizabeth Hall. *Thunder Rolling in the Mountain.*

Rand McNally Children's Atlas of Native American Cultures.

Spinka, Penina Keen. *Mother's Blessing.*

———. *White Hare's Horses.*

Thomasma, Kenneth. *Naya Nuki, Shoshoni Girl Who Ran.*

Collections

Bolden, Tonya, ed. *Rites of Passage, Stories About Growing up by Black Writers from Around the World.*

Carlson, Lori M., and Cynthia L. Ventura, eds. *Where Angels Glide at Dawn, New Stories from Latin America.*

Gallo, Donald R., ed. *Join In, Multiethnic Short Stories.*

Mazer, Anne, ed. *America Street, A Multicultural Anthology of Stories.*

Nye, Naomi Shihab, selected by. *This Same Sky, A Collection of Poems from Around the World.*

Pettepiece, Thomas, and Anatoly Aleksin, ed. *Face to Face, A Collection of Stories by Celebrated Soviet and American Writers.*

Rochman, Hazel, selected by. *Somehow Tenderness Survives, Stories of Southern Africa.*

Soto, Gary. *A Fire in My Hands, A Book of Poems.*

Strickland, Michael R., selected by. Illustrated by Alan Leiner. *Poems That Sing to You.*

Thomas, Joyce Carol, ed. *A Gathering of Flowers, Stories About Being Young in America.*

Wilson, Budge. *The Leaving and Other Stories.*

Themes and Activities

Identity

Chapter 4, Seeking a Sense of Self

Chapter 5, A Sense of Belonging

A significant aspect of growing up is the process of establishing a sense of self-awareness. This search for self is an on-going theme throughout literature, as enduring as the process of growing up itself. As we examine this theme in the context of the plurality of our society, it clearly becomes a more complex issue. Defining who we are includes understanding where we come from and gaining a heightened awareness of our cultural and ethnic heritage. While seeking a sense of self is an internal exploration, there is a related facet of this search, seeking a sense of belonging. While finding one's identity is the culmination of an internal search, the search for a sense of belonging helps the individual to see himself or herself in relationship to others and society. In Chapter 4 we examine the theme of search for identity and in Chapter 5 we examine the search for belonging.

4

Identity
Seeking a Sense of Self

As young people look for answers to the questions who am I? and where do I fit in my world? it is important to provide them with appropriate role models with whom they can identify. Research shows that young readers identify with the characters about whom they read. In looking to these role models, students can learn significant lessons about how to cope with problems, what kinds of decisions to make, and how to overcome adversity. Certainly, providing students with role models from their ethnic and social group will also help them to define their own cultural identity.

As part of the search for identity and a heightened cultural awareness, young people need to recognize and understand how to combat both racial and gender stereotyping and incidents of bias against groups and individuals. Ultimately, as students gain a sense of who they are and the inherent pride that comes from recognizing their place in their community, they will also gain a greater appreciation of others and value their cultures.

Goals

As you use this chapter with your students, the following goals will provide a focus in their exploration of the theme of search for self.

- As we search for identity, we gain an understanding of ourselves and learn to value who we are.

- As we search for identity, we find role models who can help us learn to cope with the uncertainties and problems of growing up.

- As we search for identity, we develop insights about the strengths we gain from our cultural heritage.

- As we search for identity, we learn about the effects of prejudice and stereotyping.

- As we search for identity, we gain an understanding of the future and where we might be going.

Chapter Overview

The Reader Involvement Model, presented in Chapter 2, describes student experiences with the reading of literature. Central to that model is the idea of providing opportunities for students to share what they are reading with each other in a number of ways.

We have included a number of opportunities for students to share their reactions, thoughts, and feelings with one another through journals, role playing, creative projects, and discussions. Sharing their reactions, thoughts, and feelings is an on-going process for students as they read multicultural literature to explore diversity.

In this chapter, the theme of seeking identity: a sense of self will be explored in a number of ways. First, we examine a series of quotes from focus books (In Their Own Words) that are related to the theme. Following this are Initiating Experiences. This is designed to create reader interest in the theme. This process of initiating is the first stage of the Reader Involvement Model.

In the next section, Reading and Connecting Experiences, we explore the theme of identity: a sense of self and focus on specific titles in which that theme is a significant part of the book. We begin with picture books, focusing on one specific picture book and recommending others. We then use fiction and nonfiction to examine the theme. The discussion of each individual book, picture book or novel, is followed by Responding Activities, an opportunity for student involvement. These activities, while focused on specific books, are designed to help students become involved with their reading by responding in ways that helps them to feel connected to the work. This sense of connection represents the kind of response that occurs in the second stage of the Reader Involvement Model.

After students have read the book(s) on the theme, they need additional opportunities to interact more fully with the books so that they will internalize their understanding. The follow-up activities are entitled Reflecting and Internalizing. These help readers move on to other titles, building on their understanding and experiences with their reading. These processes correspond to the third stage of the response model. Cross-curricular connections are made in the section Connections Across the Curriculum. Finally, the chapter concludes with a listing of other books, Further Reading.

In Their Own Words

The theme of identity: seeking a sense of self, as well as each of the themes that we discuss in this book, is explored in various ways by the focus books. Presenting quotations related to the theme or from the literature your students will be reading is an excellent way to get students thinking and talking about the topic. The following examples relate to diversity and the search for identify.

In this book, we are using these quotes as a type of initiating experience; however, there are a number of other ways that quotes can be used to heighten student involvement with their reading. Among the other ways that quotes can be used in the classroom are as a preview by having students speculate about the theme before they read the book; or as a focusing tool as they are reading; or as a post-reading discussion or writing prompt.

The future holds nothing but uncertainty for me, yet perhaps that is the true state of life—and I rejoice at the adventure that lies ahead.

Matas, C. *Sworn Enemies.* 1993, p. 132.

"If I had my license, I could drive," she said. "Don't be in a hurry to grow up," Iris said bitterly "Believe me, it's not worth it."

Robinson, Margaret A. *A Woman of Her Tribe.* 1990, p. 136.

Mum had told her that her father had enlisted because of school. He had wanted a way into the world for himself. Surely he would have wanted it for her, too. She wanted it for herself. She didn't know if she could do it. But she wanted to try.

Robinson, Margaret A. *A Woman of Her Tribe.* 1990, p. 144.

I cry at night sometimes. My father says, "What are you doing?" I say, " Nothing. Nothing." I get real confused.

Bode, J. *New Kids in Town, Oral Histories of Immigrant Teens.* 1989, p. 66.

Once in my English class, where I sit, someone had left me this long letter. It was in Korean and filled with curses. I couldn't believe it. It said, "Who do you think you are? Someone special? Don't be snotty."

Bode, J. *New Kids in Town, Oral Histories of Immigrant Teens.* 1989, p. 80.

I'm becoming an American and my parents are afraid of that. I try to reassure them. I tell them, "Look, it's me. You may not always know me, but I'm still me."

Bode, J. *New Kids in Town, Oral Histories of Immigrant Teens.* 1989, p. 85.

Grown-ups heard your words, but they did not listen to you.

Hiçyilmaz, G. *Against the Storm.* 1990, p. 9.

"Jonatan, I have to come, because I learn something now. Not from my family, not from the American. Just by living."

Crew, L. *Children of the River.* 1989, p. 212.

Be proud and respected as a
person, be proud in what you
are and what you may
become in the future.

From the poem "A Trail Not Yet Finished" by Priscilla
Badonie in Hirschfelder and Singer's *Rising Voices,
Writings of Young Native Americans.* 1992, p. 11.

Initiating Experiences

The following suggestions are intended to use with students to initiate the theme study. They are designed to help students to relate to the theme, to activate their prior knowledge, and to arouse their interest in it. To help students become involved with their reading we suggest varied types of experiences, including oral activities or discussions, and writing experiences. These activities are related to the initiating stage of the Reader Involvement Model.

- Prepare a 3 minute speech introducing yourself, focusing on the characteristics you have that you like.

- Bring to school a photograph of yourself when you first started school at age 5 or 6. In what ways have you changed? How are you the same?

- What character from books you have read or films or television programs you have seen is most like you? In what ways are you alike? In what ways are you different?

- Draw or create a self-portrait.

- Briefly speculate about what you will be doing in 5 years, 10 years, and 20 years.

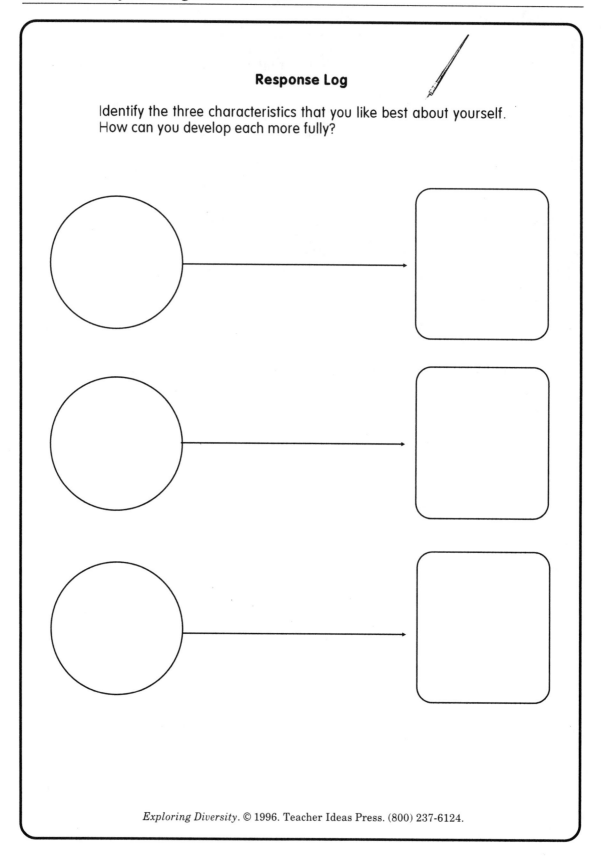

Response Log

Identify the three characteristics that you like best about yourself.
How can you develop each more fully?

Reading and Connecting Experiences

Picture Book

Picture books that illustrate the search for identity can be used effectively with older students to introduce them to a topic or to initiate class discussion.

Mochizuki, Ken. Illustrated by Dom Lee. *Baseball Saved Us*. Lee & Low Books, 1993.

This is the story of one family's experiences in the internment camps for Japanese Americans during World War II. Shorty's father senses the need to have positive recreation for the boys and men in the camp so he lays out a baseball diamond. Shorty is not very good at first, but his father tells him to try harder. He learns to be a better player, but when the family is released from the camp and goes home, he finds he is still an outsider. Eventually, baseball helps him to adjust and to be accepted.

Responding Activities. Help students to look at the illustrations in this book. Have them respond to the following: What do they contribute to the book? How do they create a sense of the camps?
See page 56.

OTHER PICTURE BOOKS

Kroll, Virginia. Illustrated by Katherine Roundtree. *Wood-Hoopoe Willie*.

Mochizuki, Ken. Illustrated by Dom Lee. *Baseball Saved Us*.

Myers, Walter Dean. *Brown Angels, An Album of Pictures and Verse*.

Say, Allen. *Grandfather's Journey*.

Rylant, Cynthia. Illustrated by Barry Moser. *Appalachia, The Voices of Sleeping Birds*.

Focus Books

Focus books are ones in which the theme of Who am I?, a seeking of a sense of identity, is a central one to the book. These are books that have broad appeal and might be read and enjoyed by most students. We recommend that you select one or more of these titles for large group or whole class study.

Buss, Fran Leeper with the assistance of Daisy Cubias. *Journey of the Sparrows*. New York: Dell Yearling, 1991. 155 pages.

For Maria, her younger brother, Oscar, and her older sister, Julia, who is expecting a child, the trip to the United States is difficult as they are smuggled across the border in a crate in the back of a truck. But life was worse at home in El Salvador where their father and Julia's husband had both been killed. Their mother and young sister had escaped to Mexico with them, but they are both ill and remain behind as the others fled to Chicago. Along with Maria and her family, a fourth person is nailed in the crate. Once in Chicago, the young people are in constant fear of the immigration workers and are vulnerable to exploitation by unscrupulous employers. For Maria, it is difficult because she is responsible for her family, yet she is also trying to establish herself in the new country.

The traditional definition of heroic would probably not be applied to Maria; however, help students to view her sense of responsibility and loyalty to her family as acts of selflessness and courage.

Responding Activities. See page 57.

Carter, Alden. *Dogwolf*. Scholastic, 1994. 231 pages.

For Pete LaSavage, it's a difficult summer. The weather is extremely hot and dry, and there are fires constantly smoldering in the peat of the federal forest. The community is poised to leave if the big fire breaks out. The heat and the fires are made even worse by the howling of his neighbor's dogwolf. But Pete's difficulties go beyond the weather. He is struggling with himself and his place in his world. He is a mix of French and Native American and moves between both cultures but doesn't feel totally at home in either. The howling dogwolf, an animal of unknown origin, further complicates the issue. Pete identifies with the animal on one level, while on another he wants it destroyed. He releases it from its cage and then must deal with the consequences as he seeks his sense of self.

One of the powerful elements of the book is Carter's description. Help students to look at the images. How does he create a sense of anxiety and danger? Teachers should carefully preview this book for its strong language and suitability.

Responding Activities. See page 58.

Crew, Linda. *Children of the River*. Dell, 1989. 213 pages.

Sundara fled from the Khmer Rouge in Cambodia. She came to the United States with her aunt's family. The family tries to hold on to the old ways that were used in Cambodia. Sundara is caught between two cultures, especially when she becomes interested in a classmate who is a star football player. She must reconcile her past with her life in the United States.

An understanding of *Children of the River* will be enhanced if readers recognize that Sundara's life is influenced by the conflict between cultures. As students read they should look for this conflict and its effect on her as well as on those around her.

Responding Activities. See page 59.

Hamilton, Virginia. *Plain City*. Scholastic, 1993. 193 pages.

Buhlaire Sims is almost thirteen and the product of a bi-racial marriage, but she believes that her father died when she was young. Buhlaire is very much like her mother, but her skin is lighter and her hair straw-colored. She is struggling to try to make sense out of her life. Curious about her identity, she discovers that her father is in fact alive. She knows that her father is white, but she wants to know about him and about her heritage.

The strong character of Buhlaire is a significant source of motivation in the book. Have students look for how she handles the difficulties she encounters and how she accepts the revelations about her family.

Responding Activities. See page 60.

Okimoto, Jean Davies. *Molly by Any Other Name.* Scholastic, 1990. 276 pages.

Molly Lane Fletcher has everything going for her. She has made the cheerleading squad, things are going well at school, she has many friends, and her parents are very loving and supportive. But something is missing. Molly is adopted and she longs to know who she really is. Her confusion about her adoption is compounded by the fact that hers is an interracial adoption and she wanted to know about her Asian roots.

This is a book about a quest. Help students to understand the literal and figurative nature of Molly's need to know about her birth parents. As students read *Molly by Any Other Name,* have them explore her relationships. Molly has a very supportive family, but they are reluctant for her to seek her birth mother. Help students to understand how the people in her life respond to her quest. Have them discuss what the book's title means.

Responding Activities. See page 61.

Salisbury, Graham. *Blue Skin of the Sea.* Delacorte Press, 1992. 215 pages.

Eleven interrelated stories describe the life of Sonny Mendoza, a Hawaiian boy, and his family from age six until his graduation from high school. Interwoven in the narratives are the rich family life, Sonny's struggle to understand himself and his past, and the overwhelming presence of the sea with its beauty and its dangers.

In reading this book, help students to focus on the images that Salisbury creates to help the reader visualize the island of Hawaii. Have students think about what makes the setting unique. As much as Sonny and his family are characters in this book, so is the ocean. As with any character, the sea has facets and it is changeable. Have students collect passages that demonstrate the character of the sea.

Responding Activities. See page 62.

Wolff, Virginia Euwer. *Probably Still Nick Swansen.* Henry Holt & Co., 1988. 144 pages.

Nick Swansen is sixteen and in high school, but he is in the "special" room, Room 19, for students with learning problems. Nick wrestles with some of the same feelings and needs and problems as other teenagers, but these are exacerbated by the unwritten rules that govern what is acceptable and unacceptable behavior for special education students. Nick struggles with his need for independence and with troubling memories of his sister's death.

The character development of Nick is significant in this book. Help students to see how the author develops his character. Also have them observe how he is different from the way people initially assume he is.

Responding Activities. See page 63.

Response Log:
Baseball Saved Us

Relate an experience that you have had when you felt that you did
not belong with the group. What did you do? How did you feel?

Response Log:
Journey of the Sparrows

Reflect on the experience that Maria and the others had in Chicago. Discuss how she grew and gained a sense of identity in the face of difficulties.

Response Log:
Dogwolf

Put yourself in Pete's position. Would you have freed the dogwolf? Why or why not?

Response Log:
Children of the River

As Sundara becomes acclimated to life in the United States, she reacts to the traditions from her country. List the traditions that are presented in the book and then briefly discuss Sundara's reaction.

Khmer Tradition	Sundara's Reactions/Actions

Response Log:
Plain City

Use the following character chart to examine Buhlaire's relationship with her father by tracing her knowledge about him and her reactions about it. In each box describe the information that Buhlaire has about her father. For each of the pieces of information, then add how she reacted in the circle directly below each box. Once you have completed the chart, then briefly describe how Buhlaire has gained a sense of who she is through her encounter with her father.

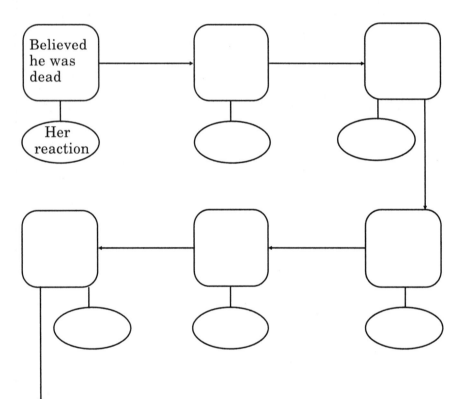

Response Log:
Molly by Any Other Name

This book raises an interesting question: what's in a name? Write your full names on a sheet of paper. Then research the meaning of your first, middle, and last names. Ask your parents why they selected the names that they did and find out who, if anyone, you were named for.

Response Log:
Blue Skin of the Sea

Using the chapters of this book as a model, reflect on your experiences and create a "chapter" of your life at 5, at 10, and now.

Reflection Log:
Probably Still Nick Swansen

Who is Nick Swansen?

List his characteristics:

How is Nick seen from the following perspectives?

By himself	By his parents	By others

Reflecting and Internalizing Experiences

In this section, we have selected activities to help students to respond and reflect upon books that they have read. The activities are designed to be general enough so that they can be applied to a number of different books rather than used with only a specific one. These activities can also be modified and adapted to be applied to specific books.

Use the following suggestions with students to aid them in responding to the books they are reading or to help students to reflect upon the theme and to extend their understanding of it. These experiences are varied, including oral activities or discussions, either small group or whole class; writing experiences in Reflection Logs; and exploration or creative activities, either small group or individual. These activities are designed to help students to internalize their reading and are related to the internalizing stage of the Reader Involvement Model. While some of the activities may include more than one of these types, each will be categorized according to the emphasis of student activity.

- In small groups, think about the characters in the books you have been reading. Describe which ones you think are accurately portrayed and why. Are there some characters who seem to be stereotypes? What makes you think so?

- Read a biography or autobiography of a person who overcame prejudice to succeed. Prepare a brief presentation for the class, focusing on the kinds of discrimination they faced and what they did to overcome it.

- In Their Shoes: This is a form of role playing that helps you to identify with and understand characters. Select a character with either a positive or negative image from your reading. Assume the role of the character in responding to a number of situations. For example, you are unfairly accused of cheating. Or all alone, you find a briefcase with $5,000 in cash and negotiable bonds. In a group, develop situations to respond to for everyone's characters (Brown and Stephens, 1995, p. 258).

- Keep a diary in the voice of one of your favorite characters or one that you identify with the most.

- Keep a Dialogue Journal in which you have written conversations with another student about what each of you is reading.

- Use some of the selections in *Rising Voices, Writings of Young Native Americans* selected by Hirschfelder and Singer as a springboard for your writing. Write a selection that tells how you feel about your life.

- After reading about someone from a different culture or ethnic group, think about ways in which both of you are the same. Make a list of the similarities.

- Draw an artistic representation of a character as you think he or she looks.

- Design a cover jacket for a book you especially like.

- Design a sweatshirt, T-shirt, scarf, or tie based on a character with whom you identified or a book that had significance for you.

- With another class member, write a song based on one of the characters or the conflict in a book you especially liked.

CONNECTIONS ACROSS THE CURRICULUM

Students can increase their depth and breadth of understanding when they have opportunities to make connections among various content areas. The following suggestions are designed to help students relate this theme across the curriculum.

Social Studies

- Research a famous person whose ethnic heritage played a significant role in his or her achievements.

Math

- Find the population demographics of the United States, your state, and your city or town. Develop a comparison graph.

The Arts

- Research the life of an artist whose work you enjoy. How has that individual's work been influenced by his or her ethnicity?

Further Reading

These titles relate to the theme of this chapter and could be used for whole class, small group, or individual reading.

Across Cultures

Bode, Janet. *New Kids in Town, Oral Histories of Immigrant Teens.*

Lord, Bette Bao. *In the Year of the Boar and Jackie Robinson.*

Spinelli, Jerry. *Maniac Magee.*

Wolff, Virginia Euwer. *Make Lemonade.*

African American

Cornell, Jean Gay. *Louis Armstrong, Ambassador Satchmo.*

Ferris, Jeri. *Walking the Road to Freedom: A Story About Sojourner Truth.*

Hamilton, Virginia. *Paul Robeson, The Life and Times of a Free Black Man.*

Hansen, Joyce. *Home Boy.*

Haskins, Jim. *One More River to Cross, The Stories of Twelve Black Americans.*

———. *Outward Dreams, Black Inventors and Their Inventions.*

Krug, Elisabeth. *Thurgood Marshall, Champion of Civil Rights.*

Larsen, Rebecca. *Paul Robeson: Hero Before His Time.*

Lester, Julius. *Long Journey Home.*

Levine, Ellen. *Freedom's Children, Young Civil Rights Activists Tell Their Own Stories.*

McCurdy, Michael, edited and illustrated by. *Escape from Slavery, The Boyhood of Frederick Douglass in His Own Words.*

McKissack, Particia C., and Fredrick McKissack. *Madame C. J. Walker.*

———. *Sojourner Truth, Ain't I a Woman?*

McKissack, Particia C., and Fredrick McKissack, Jr. *Black Diamond, The Story of the Negro Baseball Leagues.*

Moore, Eva. *The Story of George Washington Carver.*

Myers, Walter Dean. *Malcolm X, By Any Means Necessary.*

———. *Scorpions.*

———. *Somewhere in the Darkness.*

Patterson, Charles. *Marian Anderson.*

Scheader, Catherine. *Shirley Chisholm: Teacher and Congresswoman.*

Sterling, Dorothy. *Freedom Train, The Story of Harriet Tubman.*

Williams-Garcia, Rita. *Blue Tights.*

———. *Fast Talk on a Slow Train.*

Asia

Choi, Sook Nyul. *Echoes of the White Giraffe.*

Garland, Sherry. *Song of the Buffalo Boy.*

Asian American

Garland, Sherry. *Shadow of the Dragon.*

Lee, Marie. *Finding My Voice.*

Namioka, Lensey. *April and the Dragon Lady.*

Petti, Jayne. *My Name Is San Ho.*

Caribbean Islands

Taylor, Theordore. *The Cay.*

———. *Timothy of the Cay, A Prequel-Sequel.*

Central America

Moeri, Louise. *The Forty-Third War.*

European American

Cole, Brock. *Celine.*

Conly, Jane Leslie. *Crazy Lady.*

Crutcher, Chris. *The Crazy Horse Electric Game.*

Naylor, Phyllis Reynolds. *Send No Blessing.*

European Immigrant

Nixon, Joan Lowery. *Land of Hope.*

Hawaiian American

Stanley, Fay. *The Last Princess: The Story of Ka'iolani of Hawai'i.*

Inuit

George, Jean Craighead. *Julie of the Wolves.*

———. *Water Sky.*

Jewish

Semel, Nava. Translated by Semour Simckes. *Becoming Gershona.*

Mexico

Beatty, Patricia. *Lupita Manana.*

McColley, Kevin. *The Walls of Pedro Garcia.*

Palacios, Argentia. *Viva Mexico! The Story of Benito Juarez and Cinco de Mayo.*

Mexican American

Anaya, Rudolfo. *Bless Me, Ultima.*

Bethancout, T. Ernesto. *The Me Inside of Me.*

Krumgold, Joseph. *. . . And Now Miguel.*

Roberts, Maurice. *Henry Cisneros: A Leader for the Future.*

Soto, Gary. *Living up the Street.*

———. *Local News.*

———. *Small Faces.*

———. *Taking Sides.*

Middle East

Staples, Suzanne Fisher. *Shabanu, Daughter of the Wind.*

Native American

Ferris, Jeri. *Native American Doctor: The Story of Susan LaFlesche Picotte.*

Hirschfelder, Arlene, and Beverly R. Singer, selected by. *Rising Voices, Writings of Young Native Americans.*

Hobbs, Will. *Beardance.*

————. *Bearstone.*

Munson, Sammye. *Our Tejano Heroes: Outstanding Mexican-Americans in Texas.*

Naylor, Phyllis Reynolds. *To Walk the Sky Path.*

Pitts, Paul. *Shadowman's Way.*

Robinson, Margaret A. *A Woman of Her Tribe.*

Russia

Matas, Carol. *Sworn Enemies.*

South Africa

Gordon, Shelia. *Waiting for the Rain.*

Turkey

Hiçyilmaz, Gaye. *Against the Storm.*

Collections

Bolden, Tonya, ed. *Rites of Passage, Stories About Growing up by Black Writers from Around the World.*

Carlson, Lori M., and Cynthia L. Ventura, eds. *Where Angels Glide at Dawn, New Stories from Latin America.*

Gallo, Donald R., ed. *Join In, Multiethnic Short Stories.*

Mazer, Anne, ed. *America Street, A Multicultural Anthology of Stories.*

Nye, Naomi Shihab, selected by. *This Same Sky, A Collection of Poems from Around the World.*

Pettepiece, Thomas, and Anatoly Aleksin, ed. *Face to Face, A Collection of Stories by Celebrated Soviet and American Writers.*

Rochman, Hazel, selected by. *Somehow Tenderness Survives, Stories of Southern Africa.*

Soto, Gary. *A Fire in My Hands, A Book of Poems.*

Strickland, Michael R., selected by. Illustrated by Alan Leiner. *Poems That Sing to You.*

Thomas, Joyce Carol, ed. *A Gathering of Flowers, Stories About Being Young in America.*

Wilson, Budge. *The Leaving and Other Stories.*

5

Identity
A Sense of Belonging

Keziah

I have a secret place to go.
Not anyone may know.

And sometimes when my mother
Is scolding my big brother,

My secret place, it seems to me,
Is quite the only place to be.

Gwendolyn Brooks

While young people need to acquire a sense of themselves and their relationships with their family and peers, there is another facet to their sense of connectedness. They also seek a sense of belonging that can be manifested in a number of ways. On the most basic level a sense of belonging means that that they feel that they have a place in their world where they are accepted. All people have an innate need to have a connection with a place, a physical locale, to feel that there is a place where they belong. As the Brooks poem demonstrates, such a place may be a private escape. For some it may be in the idea of home while for others it might be in an idealized projection of what they would like their lives to be like. A sense of place may also be a house or it may be a town, city, state, or country. It also may be less concrete, for it may be in the mind or the imagination of the seeker. In these cases, a sense of place or a sense of belonging is a state of mind, a perspective or self-perception of individuals as they determine where they fit in their world. Whether the sense of place is an actual physical location or whether it is a state of mind, it is an essential awareness that young people must have to see themselves in relationship to their world.

Goals

As you use this chapter with your students, the following goals will provide a focus in their exploration of the theme of sense of belonging.

- As we seek a sense of belonging, we gain an understanding of ourselves and our heritage, and learn to value who we are.

- As we seek a sense of belonging, we seek a place where we belong.

- As we seek a sense of belonging, we develop insights about ourselves in relationship to our diverse surroundings.

- As we seek a sense of belonging, we can learn about our environment.

- As we seek a sense of belonging, we can gain an understanding of our surroundings and a perspective of where we are going.

Chapter Overview

The Reader Involvement Model, presented in Chapter 2, describes student experiences with the reading of literature. Central to that model is the idea of providing opportunities for students to share what they are reading with each other in a number of ways.

We have included a number of opportunities for students to share their reactions, thoughts, and feelings with one another through journals, role playing, creative projects, and discussions. Sharing their reactions, thoughts, and feelings is an on-going process for students as they read multicultural literature to explore diversity.

In this chapter, the theme of seeking identity—a sense of belonging, a sense of place will be explored in a number of ways. First, we examine a series of quotes from focus books (In Their Own Words) that are related to the theme. Following this are Initiating Experiences. This is designed to create reader interest in the theme. This process of initiating is the first stage of the Reader Involvement Model.

In the next section, Reading and Connecting Experiences, we explore the theme of identity: a sense of belonging and focus on specific titles in which that theme is a significant part of the book. We begin with picture books, focusing on one specific picture book and recommending others. We then use fiction and nonfiction to examine the theme. The discussion of each individual book, picture book or novel, is followed by Responding Activities, an opportunity for student involvement. These activities, while focused on specific books, are designed to help students become involved with their reading by responding in ways that help them to feel connected to the work. This sense of connection represents the kind of response that occurs in the second stage of the Reader Involvement Model.

After students have read the book(s) on the theme, they need additional opportunities to interact more fully with the books so that they will internalize their understanding. The follow-up activities are entitled Reflecting and Internalizing. These help readers move on to other titles, building on their understanding and experiences with their reading. These processes correspond to the third stage of the response model. Cross-curricular connections are made in the section Connections Across the Curriculum. Finally, the chapter concludes with a listing of other books, Further Reading.

In Their Own Words

Each of the themes that we discuss in this book is explored in various ways by the focus books. Presenting quotations related to the theme or from the literature your students will be reading is an excellent way to get students thinking and talking about the topic. The following examples relate to diversity and seeking a sense of belonging, a sense of place.

In this book, we are using these quotes as a type of initiating experience; however, there are a number of other ways that quotes can be used to heightened student involvement with their reading. Among the other ways that quotes can be used in the classroom are as a preview by having students speculate about the theme before they read the book; as a focusing tool as they are reading; or as a post-reading discussion prompt.

It had taken me a while to get the picture right, to imagine Jennifer, our home, and our lives. When I'd first designed the Plan, I'd tried to picture some of the girls at school in that place in my future. But none of them had ever seemed quite right. So, I'd invented Jennifer, and she'd become real in my dreams.

Carter, A. *Up Country*. 1989, pp. 52-53.

Miss Effie must have known all along. Of course! The founder of Gumbo Grove was Alexander Morgan G. Dickson, who was buried in our cemetery. Our history. And everybody's history.

Tate, Eleanora E. *The Secret of Gumbo Grove*. 1987, p. 98.

"See this field?" Planter shielded his eyes as he looked out over the field. "There's six just like this one, but this was the first one the Lewises had. That's why they call it the Glory Field. There's been a Lewis in this field as long as anybody knowed anything about this part of the world. We were here before most white people were here."

Myers, Walter Dean. *The Glory Field*. 1994, p. 352.

That's the vision. I have put my trust in you, and I think I can do it. I have to change my thinking. Belonging is important to me, but you can't really do it until you're ready to belong."

Bennett, James. *Dakota Dream*. 1994, p. 175.

He shook his head sorrowfully. "It is hard to believe that the German people could have brought themselves to commit such crimes as they did under the Nazis. Yet they did. Sometimes people do terrible things, but we must believe that goodness in man will prevail over evil, and that your classmates can learn the difference between the two. The letter certainly proves that they can learn."

Boraks-Nemetz, Lillian. *The Old Brown Suitcase.* p. 84.

Mehmet did not understand how anyone could talk of going away in the spring. Spring was short enough: a few beautiful weeks between the melting of the last snow and the coming of a burning summer when the waist-high grasses dried and rustled and scratched.

Hiçyilmaz, G. *Against the Storm.* 1990, p. 1

Initiating Experiences

The following suggestions are intended to be used with students to initiate the theme study. They are designed to help students to relate to the theme, to activate their prior knowledge, and to arouse their interest in it. To help students become involved with their reading we suggest varied types of experiences, oral activities or discussions, and writing experiences. These activities are related to the initiating stage of the Reader Involvement Model. While some of the activities may include more than one of these types, each will be categorized according to the emphasis of student activity.

- Find a descriptive passage that creates a vivid image of a place that is special to you. Practice reading it aloud and present it to your classmates.

- In small groups design bumper stickers about either a sense of belonging or a sense of place.

Response Log

Where is that "special" place where you go when you need to be alone?

Away from your own house, where do you feel most at home?

Reading and Connecting Experiences

Picture Book

Picture books that illustrate the search for a sense of belonging, a sense of place can be used effectively with older students to introduce them to a topic or to initiate class discussion.

Knight, Mary Burns. Illustrated by Anne Sibley O'Brien. *Who Belongs Here? An American Story*. Gardiner, Maine: Tilbury House Publishers, 1993.

When Nary and his grandmother came to the United States, they were escaping from the horrors in Cambodia. While he begins to enjoy the new freedom and the experiences in his new home, some of his classmates are unkind and tell him to go back where he came from. This raises questions about who belongs here.

In this book, the author also includes information about immigration to the United States in italics at the bottom of pages. Help students to recognize how this combination of the story with information contributes to the book.

Responding Activities. See page 78.

OTHER PICTURE BOOKS

Knight, Mary Burns. Illustrated by Anne Sibley O'Brien. *Who Belongs Here?*

Say, Allen. *Grandfather's Journey*.

Brown, Tricia. Photographs by Kenneth Kobre. *L'Chaim: The Story of a Russian Emigre Boy. Russian Girl Life in an Old Russian Town*.

Joosse, Barbara M. Illustrated by Marcia Sewall. *The Morning Chair*.

Focus Books

Focus books are ones in which the theme of a sense of belonging or a sense of place, a seeking of a sense of identity, is a central one to the book. These are books that have broad appeal and might be read and enjoyed by most students. We recommend that you select one or more of these titles for large group or whole class study.

Bennett, James. *Dakota Dream*. New York: Scholastic Books, 1994. 182 pages.

After a lifetime in group homes or foster homes, Floyd Rayfield longs for a place where he feels that he belongs. He has a dream that he is destined to be a Dakota. He chooses to take a new name, Charly Black Crow. Floyd runs away from his foster home and heads for Pine Ridge Reservation where he hopes to pursue his destiny and to seek his Indian identity. Chief Bear-in-cave decides that Floyd, Charly Black Crow, needs the opportunity to seek a direction for his life. He gives Charly Black Crow the opportunity to go on an *hanblecheya,* a vision quest, in which he goes into the wilderness alone and fasts for four days and nights. This opportunity is an honor that Charly Black Crow earned by his knowledge and sincere desire to establish his sense of belonging.

As a pre-reading experience, introduce students to the Native American customs and terminology that are used in this book. Help students to gain an appreciation for other cultures by discussing Floyd's interest in Native Americans.

Responding Activities. See page 79.

Boraks-Nemetz, Lillian. *The Old Brown Suitcase: A Teenager's Story of War and Peace.* Ben-Simon Publications, 1994. 148 pages.

Slava tells the story of her family's immigration to Canada and their first two years there. The chapters about life after World War II are juxtaposed with chapters about her experiences during the war. Slava and her parents are Jewish survivors of the war. As she tells of the adjustments to a new country, a new language, and a new school experience, she remembers her life in Warsaw before the war, in the ghetto and in hiding during the war, and in Warsaw again after the war. Although she came from an educated, wealthy family, they lost everything in the war. They still struggled after the war. Slava has problems adapting to school and making new friends because she is hiding her past. She makes up a story about her past to hide her experiences in the Warsaw ghetto and later in hiding in the Polish countryside. She encounters anti-Semiticism and insensitivity, so she must make a place for herself by gaining a sense of belonging in her new home.

Boraks-Nemetz includes an introduction that gives readers an historical perspective of events in Poland during World War II. Have students do further research about the War, the Holocaust, and the treatment of Jews.

Responding Activities. See page 80.

Carter, Alden. *Up Country.* New York: G. P. Putnam's Sons Scholastic Point, 1989. 256 pages.

Carl's life is difficult. His mother is an alcoholic and Carl tries to take care of her. Carl is very bright and has a gift for electronics. When a classmate brings him a car stereo in need of repairs, Carl realizes that it is stolen. He becomes involved in a lucrative, but illegal, stolen car radio business. He does not steal the stereos and radios, but he repairs and boxes the stolen goods so that they can be resold. For Carl, the money that he makes will provide him with a way out of his dismal life. He invents a world that he will escape to when he is grown up and gets an education, but he needs money to go to college. He wants to be an electrical engineer, with lots of money. He envisions a perfect life to make up for his life with his mother. When his mother is sent to a detoxification program, Carl is sent up country to live with relatives, his aunt, uncle, and cousin that he hardly knows. Suddenly, Carl has a family with new expectations and responsibilities. Life on the farm up country is far removed from the life he had in the city. When his accomplices in the stolen car radio business are caught, Carl must return home to face charges. Then Carl must decide where he belongs.

The development of Carl as a believable character is an important element to this story. Help students to focus on the changes that he goes through as they read and discuss this book.

Responding Activities. See page 81.

Hiçyilmaz, Gaye. *Against the Storm.* Bantam Doubleday Dell Publishing Group, Inc. New York: Yearling Book, 1990. 200 pages.

Life is tough in the country so Mehmet's family decides to move to Ankara to find a better life. Mehmet, a young Turkish boy, is happy in his village and does not want to leave. His parents are determined to make a better life in the city, but they soon find out that life is even harder there than in the country. The family stays in an apartment in an unfinished building belonging to Mehmet's uncle. His uncle is wealthy and owns property in shantytown. He offers poorly paying jobs to Mehmet's father and sister. The more difficult life becomes for the family, the more Mehmet is left to take care of himself. In addition to all the other challenges that face Mehmet, he also has to deal with his vicious cousin, Hakan, who flaunts his wealth and is mean to everyone. Mehmet becomes friends with a resourceful orphan named Muhlis who is a junkman, buying and selling things that he finds. The boys are drawn together by their shared love of their animals. Mehmet has a dog, Korsan, that he had brought from the country with him and Muhlis cares for his brother's horse while he is in the army. They became close friends and Mehmet helps Mulis in his work. As Mehmet's family suffers under the stress of living in the city, he becomes increasingly independent and begins to make decisions about taking control of his life. He seeks a place where he will be able to make a home for himself.

Have your students examine the idea of making choices in this book. Help them to relate this to making choices in their lives.

Responding Activities. See page 82.

Myers, Walter Dean. *The Glory Field.* New York: Scholastic Books, 1994. 375 pages.

This is the story of five generations of the Lewis family, African Americans who came here as slaves in the late 18th century. The early generations of the family were kept as slaves working on the Live Oaks Plantation, Curry Island, South Carolina. After the Civil War, the Yankees divided up land among Blacks who wished to stay in the South. The Lewis family was given eight acres adjoining Live Oaks to farm. Subsequent generations left the South and settled in Chicago or New York, but the Glory Field stayed in the family and was the root of the family.

The Glory Field is more than just a place to the Lewis family. Help students to discover what it means to the family. Have them focus on its significance and the role it plays in the novel.

Responding Activities. See page 83.

Salisbury, Graham. *Under the Blood-Red Sun*. Delacorte Press, 1994. 246 pages.

Tomi is growing up in Hawaii. He is an American, but his parents and grandfather are from Japan. His grandfather holds on to the traditions of his home land and considers himself to still be Japanese. When Grandpa hangs the Japanese flag on the clothes line, Tomi and his friend Billy make him hide it. After all in 1941, national loyalty is an issue. Tomi's family reluctantly accepts Billy because he is a *haole,* a white boy. Race, culture, and tradition are of little importance to the boys. Baseball is their interest. Billy is a pitcher and Tomi, his catcher. For Tomi, life changes abruptly on December 7 when the Japanese bomb Pearl Harbor. Grandpa waved the Japanese flag when the bombers flew over their house to protect them from harm, but a neighbor saw it and reported him as aiding the enemy. Tomi's father is arrested when his fishing boat returns to shore and shortly afterwards so is Grandpa. Unlike his father and grandfather, Tomi's loyalties have always been with his home in the islands, the only home he had ever known. But being a Japanese or even a Japanese American in Hawaii is not easy during the War.

The treatment of Japanese Americans during World War II is a shameful chapter in our history and one about which students frequently know little. Provide students with a sense of the historical background of the time.

Responding Activities. See page 84.

Soto, Gary. *Taking Sides*. Orlando: Harcourt Brace Jovanovich, 1991. 138 pages.

Lincoln Mendoza is going to a new school. His mother moved from the barrio to a suburban neighborhood that she thought would be a safer place to bring Linc up. But Linc wishes that they were back in the barrio where his friends are and where he was at home. Linc encounters prejudice and misconceptions in his new neighborhood. Only playing basketball keeps Linc happy; however, his loyalties are tested when his new school is scheduled to play basketball against his old school. Linc struggles to figure out where he belongs.

While the basketball game is one type of conflict that Lincoln experiences in this book, help students to recognize that the primary conflict is the internal one that Linc feels. Guide students to distinguish between internal and external conflicts in their reading and in their daily lives.

Responding Activities. See page 85.

Tate, Eleanora E. *The Secret of Gumbo Grove*. New York: Bantam Doubleday Dell, 1988. 199 pages.

Raisin Stackhouse likes history, but she wonders why the only history she learns in school is about the white folks and there is nothing about any Black people. She helps old Miss Effie Pfluggins with odd jobs including helping to clean up the old cemetery at the church. In return, Miss Effie shares the church records with her. Between the records and Miss Effie, Raisin gets a living history lesson.

Every community has a unique history. Help students to recognize the history of their community and how it contributes to the residents' sense of place.

Responding Activities. See page 86.

Response Log:
Who Belongs Here?

The book poses a serious question. How do you respond to who belongs here?

Response Log:
Dakota Dream

A vision quest is a sacred Native American experience. Research
this tradition and prepare a report about it.

Response Log:
The Old Brown Suitcase

Imagine that you have to leave your home on short notice. What would you pack in your suitcase?

Response Log:
Up Country

Plot the major events that occur in the story and the effect that each has on Carl. A plotline traces the action of a story, ascending and declining according to the events. On the line an X marks the major actions. Label the events on the plotline.

Response Log:
Against the Storm

Assume that two years have passed since the end of the book. Using Mehmet's point of view, write about what his life is like.

Response Log:
The Glory Field

Select one of the generations of the Lewis family and write the next chapter in his or her life.

Response Log:
Under the Blood-Red Sun

Circumstances make it difficult for Tomi to feel that he belongs. Select an incident in the book when his sense of belonging is challenged. Imagine that you are experiencing the situation. Write a diary entry discussing how you feel.

Taking Sides
Discussion Continuum

The discussion continuum is a strategy for involving all students in a lively discussion. The teachers draw a continuum on the board with opposing statements at either end point. They have students write their initials somewhere along the continuum on the spot that best specifies their position on the issue. During the following discussion, the students explain their positions, often using references from their reading to back up their points. The only rules are that everyone must have a chance to speak before anyone can speak for a second time and that all positions must be listened to respectfully. Initially, teachers may structure the discussion so that students representing views at opposite ends of the continuum alternate speaking. It is our experience, however, that once students get involved, they take over the discussion themselves and are soon responding to each other rather than using the teacher as the person who must keep the discussion going. It is also our experience that some students decide to change their position and thus their place on the continuum as a result of the discussion.

The discussion continuum works well as a springboard for writing or for further research on an issue or creative project. As students become familiar with the discussion continuum, they can create their own opposing statements in small groups or individually. Having students create their own statements helps them to develop critical thinking skills and to internalize what they are reading at a deeper level. The following is an example of a discussion continuum (Stephens and Brown, 1994, p.680-81, Brown and Stephens, 1995, p.82).

Linc should not have played against his old team	Linc should have played against his old team

Response Log:
The Secret of Gumbo Grove

Go to the oldest cemetery in your area. What do you learn about this area? Write a report or create a story based on the information you have found.

Exploring Diversity. © 1996. Teacher Ideas Press. (800) 237-6124.

Reflecting and Internalizing Experiences

In this section, we have selected activities to help students respond to and reflect upon books that they have read or that they will read. The activities are designed to be general enough so that they can be applied to a number of different books rather than used with only a specific one. These activities can also be modified and adapted to be applied to specific books.

Use the following suggestions with students to aid them in responding to the books they are reading or to help students to reflect upon the theme and to extend their understanding of it. These experiences are varied, including oral activities or discussions, either small group or whole class; writing experiences in Reflection Logs; and exploration or creative activities, either small group or individual. These activities are designed to help students to internalize their reading and are related to the internalizing stage of the Reader Involvement Model. While some of the activities may include more than one of these types, each will be categorized according to the emphasis of student activity.

- Write a one minute commercial for a special place.

- Role play a situation with a partner in which one of you is a new person without any friends or a sense of belonging. The other person tries to help make the new person feel welcome.

- Select one of the characters you have read about. How does that character create a sense of belonging?

- Write about when you don't feel that you belong. How do you overcome this feeling?

- Do a photo essay about a place that is special to you.

- Create a map of the setting of one of the books you have read.

CONNECTIONS ACROSS THE CURRICULUM

Students can increase their depth and breadth of understanding when they have opportunities to make connections among various content areas. The following suggestions are designed to help students relate this theme across the curriculum.

Social Studies

- History is filled with incidences of conflicts over territory. Select a conflict over land and research it.

Geography

- Identify and do research on a place where you have always wanted to go. Present your findings to the class.

The Arts

• Draw a picture of a place that has been special to you.

Further Reading

These titles relate to the theme of this chapter and could be used for whole class, small group, or individual reading.

Across Cultures

Bode, Janet. *New Kids in Town, Oral Histories of Immigrant Teens.*

Lord, Bette Bao. *In the Year of the Boar and Jackie Robinson.*

Spinelli, Jerry. *Maniac Magee.*

Wolff, Virginia Euwer. *Make Lemonade.*

African American

Cornell, Jean Gay. *Louis Armstrong, Ambassador Satchmo.*

Ferris, Jeri. *Walking the Road to Freedom: A Story About Sojourner Truth.*

Hamilton, Virginia. *Paul Robeson, The Life and Times of a Free Black Man.*

Hansen, Joyce. *Home Boy.*

Haskins, Jim. *One More River to Cross, The Stories of Twelve Black Americans.*

———. *Outward Dreams, Black Inventors and Their Inventions.*

Krug, Elisabeth. *Thurgood Marshall, Champion of Civil Rights.*

Larsen, Rebecca. *Paul Robeson: Hero Before His Time.*

Lester, Julius. *Long Journey Home.*

Levine, Ellen. *Freedom's Children, Young Civil Rights Activists Tell Their Own Stories.*

McCurdy, Michael, edited and illustrated by. *Escape from Slavery, The Boyhood of Frederick Douglass in His Own Words.*

McKissack, Particia C., and Fredrick McKissack. *Madame C. J. Walker.*

———. *Sojourner Truth, Ain't I a Woman?*

McKissack, Particia C., and Fredrick McKissack, Jr. *Black Diamond, The Story of the Negro Baseball Leagues.*

Moore, Eva. *The Story of George Washington Carver.*

Myers, Walter Dean. *Malcolm X, By Any Means Necessary.*

———. *Scorpions.*

———. *Somewhere in the Darkness.*

Patterson, Charles. *Marian Anderson.*

Scheader, Catherine. *Shirley Chisholm: Teacher and Congresswoman.*

Sterling, Dorothy. *Freedom Train, The Story of Harriet Tubman.*

Williams-Garcia, Rita. *Blue Tights.*

———. *Fast Talk on a Slow Train.*

Asia

Choi, Sook Nyul. *Echoes of the White Giraffe.*

Garland, Sherry. *Song of the Buffalo Boy.*

Asian American

Garland, Sherry. *Shadow of the Dragon.*

Lee, Marie. *Finding My Voice.*

Namioka, Lensey. *April and the Dragon Lady.*

Petti, Jayne. *My Name Is San Ho.*

Caribbean Islands

Taylor, Theodore. *The Cay.*

———. *Timothy of the Cay, A Prequel-Sequel.*

Central America

Moeri, Louise. *The Forty-Third War.*

European American

Cole, Brock. *Celine.*

Conly, Jane Leslie. *Crazy Lady.*

Crutcher, Chris. *The Crazy Horse Electric Game.*

Naylor, Phyllis Reynolds. *Send No Blessing.*

Nixon, Joan Lowery. *A Place to Belong.*

European Immigrant

Nixon, Joan Lowery. *Land of Hope.*

Hawaiian American

Stanley, Fay. *The Last Princess: The Story of Ka'iolani of Hawai'i .*

Inuit

George, Jean Craighead. *Julie of the Wolves.*

———. *Water Sky.*

Jewish

Semel, Nava. Translated by Semour Simckes. *Becoming Gershona.*

Mexico

Beatty, Patricia. *Lupita Manana.*

McColley, Kevin. *The Walls of Pedro Garcia.*

Palacios, Argentia. *Viva Mexico! The Story of Benito Juarez and Cinco de Mayo.*

Mexican American

Anaya, Rudolfo. *Bless Me, Ultima.*

Bethancout, T. Ernesto. *The Me Inside of Me.*

Krumgold, Joseph. *. . . And Now Miguel.*

Roberts, Maurice. *Henry Cisneros: A Leader for the Future.*

Soto, Gary. *Living up the Street.*

————. *Local News.*

————. *Small Faces.*

————. *Taking Sides.*

Middle East

Staples, Suzanne Fisher. *Shabanu, Daughter of the Wind.*

Native American

Ferris, Jeri. *Native American Doctor: The Story of Susan LaFlesche Picotte.*

Hirschfelder, Arlene, and Beverly R. Singer, selected by. *Rising Voices, Writings of Young Native Americans.*

Hobbs, Will. *Beardance.*

————. *Bearstone.*

Munson, Sammye. *Our Tejano Heroes: Outstanding Mexican-Americans in Texas.*

Naylor, Phyllis Reynolds. *To Walk the Sky Path.*

Pitts, Paul. *Shadowman's Way.*

Robinson, Margaret A. *A Woman of Her Tribe.*

Russia

Matas, Carol. *Sworn Enemies.*

South Africa

Gordon, Shelia. *Waiting for the Rain.*

Turkey

Hiçyilmaz, Gaye. *Against the Storm.*

Collections

Appleman, Deborah, and Margaret Appleman. *Braided Lives.*

Bolden, Tonya, ed. *Rites of Passage, Stories About Growing up by Black Writers from Around the World.*

Carlson, Lori M., and Cynthia L. Ventura, eds. *Where Angels Glide at Dawn, New Stories from Latin America.*

Gallo, Donald R., ed. *Join In, Multiethnic Short Stories.*

Mazer, Anne, ed. *America Street, A Multicultural Anthology of Stories.*

Nye, Naomi Shihab, selected by. *This Same Sky, A Collection of Poems from Around the World.*

Pettepiece, Thomas, and Anatoly Aleksin, ed. *Face to Face, A Collection of Stories by Celebrated Soviet and American Writers.*

Rochman, Hazel, selected by. *Somehow Tenderness Survives, Stories of Southern Africa.*

Soto, Gary. *A Fire in My Hands, A Book of Poems.*

Strickland, Michael R., selected by. Illustrated by Alan Leiner. *Poems That Sing to You.*

Thomas, Joyce Carol, ed. *A Gathering of Flowers, Stories About Being Young in America.*

Wilson, Budge. *The Leaving and Other Stories.*

Themes and Activities

Getting Along with Others

Chapter 6, Family

Chapter 7, Friends

As young people search for a sense of their own identity, their relationships become increasingly more important, too. Frequently these relationships are a source of much uncertainty and frustration as young people explore new roles for themselves, both within their families and with their friends and peers. This is also a time of confusion, when students often question where they fit. This uncertainty too often breeds cliques and an unwillingness to be receptive to anything or anyone that is either new or different. Unfortunately, this is also a time when prejudices seem to increase and are often expressed in a cruel manner against those who are somehow perceived as "different." In these two chapters, we present multicultural literature selected to help young people understand and accept others. Chapter 6 presents literature and activities that focus on family relationships, while Chapter 7 focuses on friendship. The overall goal is to help young people develop tolerance and understanding for others through their exploration of multicultural literature.

6

Getting Along with Others
Family

The single most significant and lasting relationships that most people have are with the members of their families. We know that the family connection is a vital one for helping people to gain a sense of belonging and well-being. In the 1970s, we witnessed a tremendous testimony to the significance of family and family heritage when Alex Hailey's *Roots* became the most popular miniseries ever presented on television. It is a fundamental human need to be connected to one's family.

As we read literature of the various ethnic groups that are woven into the fabric of American culture, we are constantly reminded that the concept of family is an expanded one and on occasion a broadly interpreted one. For example, authors Whelan, Pitts, Taylor, Soto, and Nixon all present extended families with grandparents and aunts and uncles directly involved in the characters' lives. A frequent motif in family accounts is the connection between a youth and his or her grandparent. The grandparent "teaches" or shares a sense of tradition and family with the main character. Additionally, looking at our focus books, the Logan family saga presents a two-layered idea of family. First is Cassie's strong, extended family of relatives, but the second layer involves the sense of family within the community of African Americans in their small southern town.

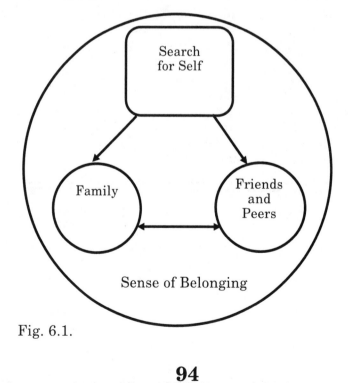

Fig. 6.1.

Goals

As you use this chapter with your students, the following goals will provide a focus in their exploration of the theme of getting along with others, the family.

- Families can provide us with a sense of connectedness and belonging.

- Families can help us to develop a sense of our own identify.

- We can relate better to family members by learning about their concerns and perspectives.

- We can relate better to people who are different from us by learning about their families and cultural heritage.

- The diversity of families contributes to the cultural richness of our society.

Chapter Overview

The Reader Involvement Model, presented in Chapter 2, describes student experiences with the reading of literature. Central to that model is the idea of providing opportunities for students to share what they are reading with each other in a number of ways.

We have included a number of opportunities for students to share their reactions, thoughts, and feelings with one another through journals, role playing, creative projects, and discussions. Sharing their reactions, thoughts, and feelings is an on-going process for students as they read multicultural literature to explore diversity.

In this chapter, the theme of getting along with others—family will be explored in a number of ways. First, we examine a series of quotes from focus books (In Their Own Words) that are related to the theme. Following this are Initiating Experiences. This is designed to create reader interest in the theme. This process of initiating is the first stage of the Reader Involvement Model.

In the next section, Reading and Connecting Experiences, we explore the theme of getting along with others: family and focus on specific titles in which that theme is a significant part of the book. We begin with picture books, focusing on one specific picture book and recommending others. We then use fiction and nonfiction to examine the theme. The discussion of each individual book, picture book or novel, is followed by Responding Activities, an opportunity for student involvement. These activities, while focused on specific books, are designed to help students become involved with their reading by responding in ways that help them to feel connected to the work. This sense of connection represents the kind of response that occurs in the second stage of the Reader Involvement Model.

After students have read the book(s) on the theme, they need additional opportunities to interact more fully with the books so that they will internalize their understanding. The follow-up activities are entitled Reflecting and Internalizing. These help readers move on to other titles, building on their understanding and experiences with their reading. These processes correspond to the third stage of the response model. Cross-curricular connections are made in the section Connections Across the Curriculum. Finally, the chapter concludes with a listing of other books, Further Reading.

In Their Own Words

Each of the themes that we discuss in this book is explored in various ways by the focus books. Presenting quotations related to the theme or from the literature your students will be reading is an excellent way to get students thinking and talking about the topic. The following examples relate to diversity and getting along with others (family).

In this book, we are using these quotes as a type of initiating experience; however, there are a number of other ways that quotes can be used to heightened student involvement with their reading. Among the other ways that quotes can be used in the classroom are as a preview by having students speculate about the theme before they read the book; or as a focusing tool as they are reading; or as a post-reading discussion prompt.

> I have made a place for myself in the circle of my family, she thought. It's still a bumpy circle and maybe Matt will always be Mama's favorite, but that's okay. At least I have a place with Mama.
>
> Boyd, C. D. *Circle of Gold*. 1984, p. 124.

> "You know what I like about your grandmom?" he asked finally. "You don't have to put on an act to impress her. You can just be what you are."
>
> Yep, L. *Child of the Owl*. 1977, p. 211.

> We have no time for a long courtship. We need no long courtship. We need each other. An urgent, burning need to rise from the ashes, to build again, fills our hearts and minds. We are alone. No family to share our joy, to tell us mazel tov, congratulations.
>
> Sender, R. *To Life*. 1988, p. 48.

> There was such a good feeling of closeness and sharing as they sat together around the big table that Yuki didn't want the day ever to end.
>
> Uchida, Y. *Journey Home*. 1978, p. 123.

> I hear Mama's voice, filled with hope. A world full of people will not be silent. We will not perish in vain. She was so sure. But she perished, and the world was silent.
>
> Sender, Ruth Minsky. *The Cage*. 1986, p. 4.

She had known little of her father's painful story. The occasion overwhelmed her and made her ache with an agony of happiness, but also with other mixed-in feelings that racked her with distress. She felt a guilt and a shame. Her father was so strong! So strong! What he believed in and did were of great substance and depth! And her values were so, so shallow! Yet she preferred hers.

Berry, J. *Ajeemah and His Son.* 1991, p. 83.

How could she follow her dreams in such a country—a place that had promised her whole family freedom, but little by little took away everything they had held dear?

Nixon, Joan Lowery. *Land of Hope.* 1992, p. 160.

Initiating Experiences

The following suggestions are intended to use with students to initiate the theme study. They are designed to help students to relate to the theme, to activate their prior knowledge, and to arouse their interest in it. In order to help students become involved with their reading we suggest varied types of experiences, oral activities or discussions, and writing experiences. These activities are related to the initiating stage of the Reader Involvement Model. While some of the activities may include more than one of these types, each will be categorized according to the emphasis of student activity.

- As a group or class, brainstorm what all families have in common regardless of their ethnic or cultural differences.

- In small groups, brainstorm as many different family configurations as you can think of, such as a single-parent father living with his children. Compare the findings of the groups. How does this information influence your definition of a family?

- Interview a member of your family. Ask that person to tell you what family life was like for him or her at your age.

- Make a collage, both impressionistic and representational, of your family.

Response Log

Describe what you think makes a family.

Response Log

Describe a tradition or custom that your family observes.

Reading and Connecting Experiences

Picture Book

Picture books that illustrate the theme of families and diversity can be used effectively with older students to introduce them to a topic or to initiate class discussion.

Polacco, Patricia. *The Keeping Quilt*. Simon & Schuster, Inc., 1988.

Patricia Polacco shares a wonderful view of her family's heritage by tracing five previous generations of her family's history and by looking ahead to her own daughter's future. Her immigrant great-great-grandmother had made a quilt for her daughter (Polacco's great-grandmother) to help her to remember their Russian heritage. The quilt is passed from generation to generation, keeping their heritage alive.

The illustrations in this book are especially important. Help your students to discover how color is used to focus on the book's meaning.

Responding Activities. See page 104.

OTHER PICTURE BOOKS

Bunting, Eve. Illustrated by Diane de Groat. *Sunshine Home*.

Bruchac, Joseph. Illustrated by Paul Morin. *Fox Song*.

Flournoy, Valerie. Illustrated by Jerry Pinkney. *The Patchwork Quilt*.

Garland, Sherry. Illustrated by Tatsuro Kiuchi. *The Lotus Seed*.

Greenfield, Eloise. Illustrated by Jan Spivey Gilchrist. *First Pink Light*.

Johnson, Angela. Illustrated by David Soman. *When I am Old with You*.

Mathis, Sharon Bell. Illustrated by Leo Dillon and Diane Dillon. *The Hundred Penny Box*.

MacLachlan, Patricia. Pictures by Pertzoff. *Three Names*.

Miles, Miska. Illustrated by Peter Parnall. *Annie and the Old One*.

Polacco, Patricia. *The Keeping Quilt*.

Stanek, Muriel. Illustrated by Judith Friedman. *I Speak English for My Mom*.

Williams, David. Illustrated by Wiktor Sadowski. *Grandma Essie's Covered*.

Focus Books

Focus books for this chapter are those in which the theme, families, is central to the book. These are books that have broad appeal and might be read and enjoyed by most students. We recommend that you select one or more of these titles for large group or whole class study.

Nixon, Joan Lowery. *Land of Hope.* Laurel Leaf Books, 1992. 171 pages.

It is said that we are a nation of immigrants and that it is immigration that has contributed significantly to our diversity. *Land of Hope,* the first of three proposed Ellis Island books, addresses the issue of coming to the United States. The story focuses upon Rebekah Levinsky and her Russian family escaping the Tsar's reign of terror against the Jews. The family joins Rebekah's uncle in New York. While life in New York turns out to be more challenging than the family expected, they all work together to make their dreams possible. On their journey Rebekah makes two friends, one from Sweden, Kristen Swensen, and the other from Ireland, Rose Carney. The three share their hopes and plans for their life in their new home. The varied backgrounds of these immigrants speaks to the rich diversity of our culture.

From the Russian countryside to life in steerage to the tenements of New York, this book provides settings in which life is difficult. While the characters experience hardships they are sustained by their hopes for a better life. The relationship among the three friends who support each others' aspirations is an major element in the book.

Responding Activities. See page 105.

Pitts, Paul. *Racing the Sun.* Avon Books, 1988. 150 pages.

Brandon has paid little attention to his Navajo heritage. His father has anglicized their family name and they live in Salt Lake City, far from the reservation. Then Brandon's grandfather comes for a visit and stays in his room. Sharing a room with the old man presents a number of challenges to the twelve year old. He must get used to the tribal customs that are a part of his grandfather's daily life. As time passes Brandon learns much of life and of his heritage from his grandfather and a strong loving relationship develops between them.

While at first his grandfather seems odd to Brandon, he comes to realize that the old man can teach him a great deal. As they read the book, help your students to focus on how Brandon's attitude changes.

Responding Activities. See page 106.

Sender, Ruth Minsky. *The Cage*. Macmillan, 1986. 245 pages.
———. *To Life*. Macmillan, 1988; Puffin Books, 1990. 229 pages.

These books, *The Cage* and its sequel, *To Life*, are the story of Ruth Minsky and her struggle to survive the Holocaust. But they are also the story of connection and strength of the family. The Nazi occupation of Poland caused hardship for all Jews. In Lodz, the Minsky family suffered as did their friends, but for teenage Ruth (Riva) the situation worsened when her mother was taken away by the Nazis. Then it was her responsibility to keep her family of three younger brothers together. They had to try to survive in the Lodz ghetto where they faced numerous obstacles, including the illness of their youngest brother. They protected him from the Nazis until he died. As conditions worsened in the ghetto, Riva and her brothers volunteered to be transported to a "work camp" in the hopes that they would be able to stay together. While life in the ghetto had been difficult, every day at Auschwitz and later at Mittelsteine was a struggle for survival. Throughout these experiences, she never gave up hope that she would be reunited with her brothers or her older sisters who were grown and had left home before the Nazi invasion. The liberation of the camps simply began a new chapter in the difficulties that Riva experienced. She had no home to return to, but she needed to find her family. Families were separated and survivors didn't know the fate of their relatives. Yet, Riva was determined to find any family that was left. *To Life* traces her struggles for the five years following the war, her marriage, her finding a few members of her family, the birth of her first two children, and their immigration to the United States.

There are many misconceptions about the Holocaust and its aftermath. Help your students to understand the Holocaust by researching the period from 1933 to 1948. Among the topics that they might look at are the political conditions in Germany that led to Hitler's gaining power; the systematic stripping of the rights and property of the Jews; the development of concentration camps; the other groups persecuted by the Nazis; the death camps; the relocation camps; and sources of aid for the refugees.

Responding Activities. See page 107.

Soto, Gary. "Baseball in April," "Two Dreamers," "Mother and Daughter," and "Growing Up," from *Baseball in April*. HBJ, 1990. 137 pages.

In these four short stories in the collection entitled *Baseball in April*, Soto presents various family relationships, such as brothers, grandfather and grandson, mother and daughter, and a girl with her family. He presents realistic pictures of growing up and the relationships that make a difference to the characters.

As your students read, have them look for similarities and differences in the relationships described in these four short stories. Help them to look for commonalties in all of the relationships and relate these to their own lives.

Responding Activities. See page 108.

Taylor, Mildred D. *Roll of Thunder, Hear My Cry.* Bantam, 1976. 210 pages.
——. *Let the Circle Be Unbroken.* Puffin Books, 1981. 394 pages.
——. *The Road to Memphis.* Dial Books, 1990. 290 pages.

The Logan family suffers through the hard days of the Depression in rural Mississippi, but they had additional challenges: they were a Black family who owned their own land. These three books trace the experiences and difficulties of the family from the 1930s to the outbreak of World War II. The books are related through the eyes of youthful Cassie Logan. The closeness of the family and their concern for one another is a crucial element in each of these books as we watch Cassie growing up.

Before your students begin reading these books, activate or develop their prior knowledge about the period that these stories cover. Understanding the racial conditions in our country during this time will enhance their understanding of the books. As your students read these books, have them discuss the growth and development of the characters and the changes that they go through.

Responding Activities. See page 109.

Whelan, Gloria. *Goodbye, Vietnam.* Alfred A. Knopf, 1992. 135 pages.

For Mai and her family survival is dependent upon their escape from their home in Vietnam. Her grandmother is an outspoken critic of the government who also tells fortunes and practices healing. It is only a matter of time before she will be arrested. The trip is arduous as they must carry their possessions and travel only at night through the Mekong Delta to get to Ho Chi Mihn City where they could board a boat for Hong Kong. The boat is old and badly over-crowded and the conditions are difficult. But the family always has hope that they will find a better life.

Help your students locate Vietnam on the map. Activate or develop their prior knowledge about the political conditions and cultural traditions of this country.

Responding Activities. See page 110.

Yep, Laurence. *The Star Fisher.* Puffin Books, 1991. 147 pages.

For the Lee family a move to West Virginia from Ohio means new opportunities. In the new town, they have bigger facilities for their laundry, the only one in town. As the only Chinese family there, they encounter some bigotry. The strong family bond gives them strength to face the problems, and they are further encouraged by some community members who also give them support.

As your students read this book, have them focus upon ways the family members relate with each other and support each other. Ask them to discuss similar experiences they may have had with their own families.

Responding Activities. See page 111.

Response Log:
The Keeping Quilt

Design a block for a quilt that represents a significant event in your family's history. Or create a quilt block focusing on an important event in the life of a family that you have read about. Once you have roughed out your design, briefly explain it.

Responding Activity:
Land of Hope

The dilemma resolution strategy focuses upon what is exciting—those instances of conflict or disharmony in books. We have found that when students ask other students to tell them "What happens next . . ?" in a book, they are not asking for a plot summary; they are asking about the action in the story. They want to know what has happened to propel the plot. For example, Elias holds true to his faith, but his brother Avir believes that work must come first. How will the brothers deal with their differing perspectives? Which position is the right one?

Using a dilemma as the focal point, student discussion can be directed to examining resolutions to the dilemmas, posing alternatives to the resolutions, or making judgments about the resolutions. The exploration that students do during this process increases their critical thinking. Using the example of Elias, questions for discussion might focus on how he might have extricated himself from debt so that he could practice both his faith and his profession. Then the situation lends itself to the discussion of a number of related issues. Is his position realistic? How will he adapt to living in a new culture? What will that mean for his family?

Response Log:
Racing the Sun

As you read, *Racing the Sun*, you will notice that the grandfather teaches Brandon many things, both Native American lore and information about nature. Make a chart in which you list the information he has learned. Then select one entry from each list and write about it.

Folklore	Nature

Response Log:
The Cage

In *The Cage*, Riva writes poetry and it helps her to survive. Write a poem about a difficult time in your life or about a challenge you have encountered.

Exploring Diversity. © 1996. Teacher Ideas Press. (800) 237-6124.

Response Log:
Gary Soto's Short Stories

These are all stories about relationships within families. Select one of these stories that you particularly enjoyed. Use it as a model to write your own short story about relationships within a family. Use the fiction map below to help you in planning the story.

Plot:

Conflict:

Major Characters:

Resolution:

Climax:

Theme:

Response Log:
The Logan Family Saga

In small groups, speculate what would happen to Cassie and her brothers subsequent to *The Road to Memphis*. Explore the time frame and develop a rough draft of a plotline. Then write letters to Mildred Taylor sharing your suggestions for the fourth book about Cassie and her family.

Response Log:
Goodbye, Vietnam

The book ends as Mai's family prepares to leave for America. Write an additional chapter using one of the following: imagine that the family has arrived in the United States, write a chapter describing their first few days in this country; or look ahead one year and write a chapter describing what their lives are like after one year in this country.

Responding Activity: *The Star Fisher*

In completing the support system chart students enter their name in the circle: my support system. Then they add to or delete from the list of descriptors of types of support. For each descriptor, the student identifies one or more people who provide them with that kind of support (named in the circles). The boxes below the circles are for students to then list ways that they feel that support.

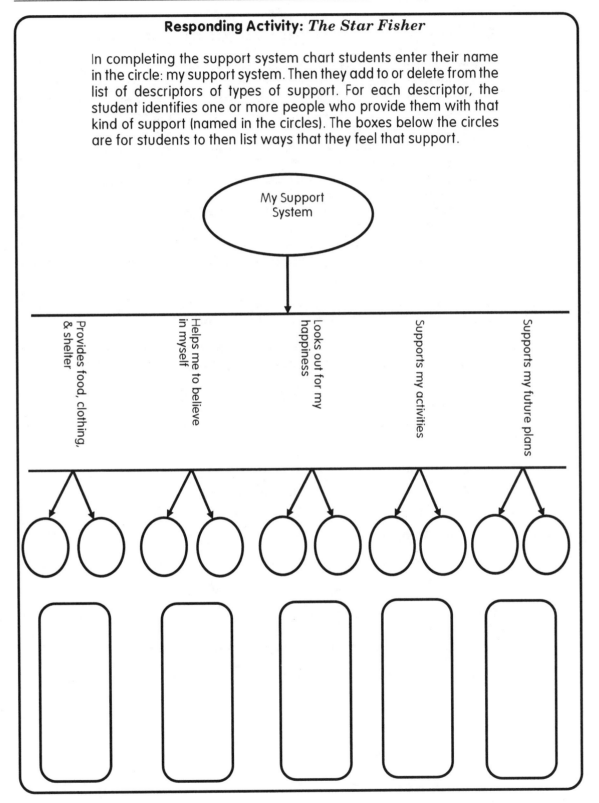

Reflecting and Internalizing Experiences

In this section, we have selected activities to help students respond to and reflect upon books that they have read or that they will read. The activities are designed to be general enough so that they can be applied to a number of different books rather than used with only a specific one. These activities can also be modified and adapted to be applied to specific books.

Use the following suggestions with students to aid them in responding to the books they are reading or to help students to reflect upon the theme and to extend their understanding of it. These experiences are varied, including oral activities or discussions, either small group or whole class; writing experiences in Reflection Logs; and exploration or creative activities, either small group or individual. These activities are designed to help students to internalize their reading and are related to the internalizing stage of the Reader Involvement Model. While some of the activities may include more than one of these types, each will be categorized according to the emphasis of student activity.

- Role play one of the events from a book you have read. Use the space below to plan the actions and dialogue for your role playing.

- Select a favorite passage from a book you have read that is about families. Practice reading it and prepare a read-aloud for your classmates.

- Plan a panel discussion with 2 to 4 other classmates in which each of you select a favorite character that you would like to have as a member of your family. Introduce him or her to the rest of the class, telling them why you feel that way.

- Write about the following:

  The most interesting family that I read about was . . .

  The family that most reminded me of my own was . . .

  When I was reading, I thought about . . .

  The part that I liked best about the book (story/poem) was . . .

  The part that I liked least about the book (story/poem) was . . .

- It's All Relative: Select a family member (preferably from a different generation such as parent, aunt, uncle, grandparent, or great-grandparent) to write a letter to describing a book you have read and liked and discussing the reasons for your reactions. Send the letter to the family member in an attempt to encourage an ongoing dialogue (from Brown and Stephens, 1995, p. 255).

- Identify an ideal or value that is significantly explored in a book and place it in a circle at the center of the map. Supporting evidence is then placed in circles and attached to the center.

Ideal/Values Map

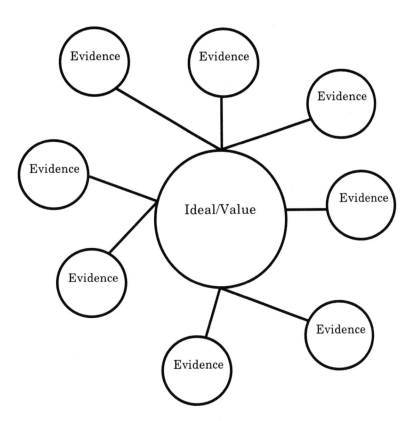

Fig. 6.2. From Brown and Stephens, 1995, pp. 248-49.

- Design a family crest depicting your family. Create a graphic with several major sections which explore aspects of the family's life. Print the family's name along the diagonal line. The other sections can be for a variety of things such as heritage, traditions, special events or activities, and family members.

- As a group or class, design and make a quilt. Have each block of the quilt represent the similarities and differences of each family in your group or class.

- Design a collage of one of the families in the books you have read.

CONNECTIONS ACROSS THE CURRICULUM

Students can increase their depth and breadth of understanding when they have opportunities to make connections among various content areas. The following suggestions are designed to help students relate this theme across the curriculum.

Social Studies

- Research the origin of family customs and traditions for your own ethnic group or for one that interests you.

Geography

- Locate on an atlas where the families you have read about lived. Trace their travels.

- Locate all the places where your family or relatives have lived.

Music

- Research the history and versions of a favorite song of your family's that is ethnic in origin.

Physical Education and Sports

- Ask some of your family members or someone in your community to tell you about a game they enjoy that has an ethnic origin.

Further Reading

These titles relate to the theme of this chapter and could be used for whole class, small group, or individual reading.

Across Cultures

Bode, Janet. *New Kids in Town, Oral Histories of Immigrant Teens.*

African American

Boyd, Candy Dawson. *Circle of Gold.*

Collier, James Lincoln, and Christopher Collier. *Who Is Carrie?*

Hamilton, Virginia. *Cousins.*

———. *The House of Dies Drear.*

Hansen, Joyce. *Home Boy.*

Johnson, Angela. *Toning the Sweep.*

Meyer, Carolyn. *White Lilacs.*

Moore, Yvette. *Freedom Songs.*

Myers, Walter Dean. *Somewhere in the Darkness.*

———. *Won't Know Till I Get There.*

Sebestyen, Ouida. *Words by Heart.*

Smothers, Ethel Footman. *Down in the Piney Woods.*

Taylor, Mildred D. *Song of the Trees.*

Wilson, Johnniece Marshall. *Oh, Brother.*

Asia

Choi, Sook Nyul. *Year of Impossible Goodbyes.*

Ho, Minfong. *The Clay Marble.*

Mori, Kyoko. *Shizuko's Daughter.*

Whelan, Gloria. *Goodbye, Vietnam.*

Asian American

Houston, Jeanne Wakatsuki, and James D. Houston. *Farewell to Manzanar.*

Howard, Ellen. *Her Own Song.*

Namioka, Lensey. *Yang the Youngest and His Terrible Ear.*

Okimoto, Jean Davies. *Molly by Any Other Name.*

Uchida, Yoshiko. *Journey Home.*

Yep, Laurence. *Child of the Owl.*

———. *Dragon's Gate.*

———. *Dragonwings.*

———. *Sea Glass.*

Caribbean Islands

Berry, James. *Ajeemah and His Son.*

Dorris, Michael. *Morning Girl.*

Eastern European

Filipovic, Zlata. Translated by Christina Pribichevich-Zoric. *Zlata's Diary, A Child's Life in Sarajevo.*

European American

Bauer, Marion Dane. *A Dream of Queens and Castles.*

———. *A Question of Trust.*

———. *A Taste of Smoke.*

———. *Face to Face.*

———. *On My Honor.*

Bridgers, Sue Ellen. *Permanent Connections.*

Carter, Alden R. *Up Country.*

MacLachlan, Patricia. *Journey.*

Mazer, Harry. *When the Phone Rang.*

Mazer, Norma Fox. *After the Rain.*

Rylant, Cynthia. *Missing May.*

Voight, Cynthia. *Dicey's Song.*

European Immigrant

Colman, Hila. *Rachel's Legacy.*

Koller, Jackie French. *Nothing to Fear.*

Nixon, Joan Lowery. *A Family Apart.*

———. *A Place to Belong.*

———. *Land of Dreams.*

——. *Land of Hope.*

——. *Land of Promise.*

Hawaiian American

Salisbury, Graham. *Blue Skin of the Sea.*

Holocaust

Isaacman, Clara, as told to Joan Adess Grossman. *Clara's Story.*

Matas, Carol. *Daniel's Story.*

Reiss, Johanna. *The Upstairs Room.*

Richter, Hans Peter. Translated from the German by Edite Kroll. *Friedrich.*

Sachs, Marilyn. *A Pocket Full of Seeds.*

Siegal, Aranka. *Upon the Head of a Goat.*

Yolen, Jane. *Devil's Arithmetic.*

Mexican American

Buss, Fran Leeper, with the assistance of Daisy Cubias. *Journey of the Sparrows.*

Meltzer, M. *The Hispanic Americans.*

Middle East

Staples, Suzanne Fisher. *Haveli.*

——. *Shabanu, Daughter of the Wind.*

Native American

Naylor, Phyllis Reynolds. *To Walk the Sky Path.*

Robinson, Margaret A. *A Woman of Her Tribe.*

Russia

Bograd, Larry. *The Kolokol Papers.*

Hautzig, Esther. *The Endless Steppe.*

Lasky, Kathryn. *The Night Journey.*

South Africa

Gordon, Shelia. *The Middle of Somewhere, A Story of South Africa.*

Collections

Bolden, Tonya, ed. *Rites of Passage, Stories About Growing up by Black Writers from Around the World.*

Carlson, Lori M., and Cynthia L. Ventura, eds. *Where Angels Glide at Dawn, New Stories from Latin America.*

Gallo, Donald R., ed. *Join In, Multiethnic Short Stories.*

Mazer, Anne, ed. *America Street, A Multicultural Anthology of Stories.*

Nye, Naomi Shihab, selected by. *This Same Sky, A Collection of Poems from Around the World.*

Pettepiece, Thomas, and Anatoly Aleksin, eds. *Face to Face, A Collection of Stories by Celebrated Soviet and American Writers.*

Rochman, Hazel, selected by. *Somehow Tenderness Survives, Stories of Southern Africa.*

Soto, Gary. *A Fire in My Hands, A Book of Poems.*

Strickland, Michael R., selected by. Illustrated by Alan Leiner. *Poems That Sing to You.*

Thomas, Joyce Carol, ed. *A Gathering of Flowers, Stories About Being Young in America.*

Wilson, Budge. *The Leaving and Other Stories.*

7

Getting Along with Others
Friends

Friendship is a complex relationship. How do friendships develop? Who becomes friends? Some people often expect that friends are much alike with similar backgrounds and interests. But friendship is not that predictable. We never can assume that two individuals will become friends because of their similarities. Other people rely on the old cliché, "opposites attract," to explain when friends are different from each other in many ways. Neither position is foolproof, nor is it an accurate gauge to predict friendships. Friendships are as diverse as society is in general. It is in the differences between friends that they each learn and grow. In a society that not only recognizes but celebrates its diversity, the ideas of differences need to be more than recognized and accepted; they need to be nurtured. Friendship is the appropriate vehicle for the nourishing of differences.

Friendship is a frequent theme in literature for young people. The friendship among characters is often the most significant relationship in this literature. Those relationships provide support for the characters; they help characters to deal with perplexing situations; and they help characters to decide where they fit in their world.

Goals

As you use this chapter with your students, the following goals will provide a focus in their exploration of getting along with others, friends.

- Friendships are important for a happy, healthy life.

- Friendships provide us with ways to learn more about ourselves.

- Friendships help us learn about people who are different from us.

- Friendships help us learn about other customs and traditions.

- Friendships teach us to respect people who are different from us.

Chapter Overview

The Reader Involvement Model, presented in Chapter 2, describes student experiences with the reading of literature. Central to that model is the idea of providing opportunities for students to share what they are reading with each other in a number of ways.

We have included a number of opportunities for students to share their reactions, thoughts, and feelings with one another through journals, role playing, creative projects, and discussions. Sharing their reactions, thoughts, and feelings is an on-going process for students as they read multicultural literature to explore diversity.

In this chapter, the theme of getting along with others—friends, will be explored in a number of ways. First, we examine a series of quotes from focus books (In Their Own Words) that are related to the theme. Following this are Initiating Experiences. This is designed to create reader interest in the theme. This process of initiating is the first stage of the Reader Involvement Model.

In the next section, Reading and Connecting Experiences, we explore the theme of getting along with others: friends and focus on specific titles in which that theme is a significant part of the book. We begin with picture books, focusing on one specific picture book and recommending others. We then use fiction and nonfiction to examine the theme. The discussion of each individual book, picture book or novel, is followed by Responding Activities, an opportunity for student involvement. These activities, while focused on specific books, are designed to help students become involved with their reading by responding in ways that help them to feel connected to the work. This sense of connection represents the kind of response that occurs in the second stage of the Reader Involvement Model.

After students have read the book(s) on the theme, they need additional opportunities to interact more fully with the books so that they will internalize their understanding. The follow-up activities are entitled Reflecting and Internalizing. These help readers move on to other titles, building on their understanding and experiences with their reading. These processes correspond to the third stage of the response model. Cross-curricular connections are made in the section Connections Across the Curriculum. Finally, the chapter concludes with a listing of other books, Further Reading.

In Their Own Words

Each of the themes that we discuss in this book is explored in various ways by the focus books. Presenting quotations related to the theme or from the literature your students will be reading is an excellent way to get students thinking and talking about the topic. The following examples relate to diversity and getting along with others (friends).

In this book, we are using these quotes as a type of initiating experience; however, there are a number of other ways that quotes can be used to heightened student involvement with their reading. Among the other ways that quotes can be used in the classroom are as a preview by having students speculate about the theme before they read the book; or as a focusing tool as they are reading; or as a post-reading discussion prompt.

From that day on Matthew was my best friend. I didn't have to stand by myself at recess anymore, and we helped each other a lot in school.

> Namioka, L. *Yang the Youngest and His Terrible Ear.*
> 1992, p. 37.

Matthew pretended not to hear, but his face turned a little red. For the first time, I realized that being friends with me could be embarrassing for him. But that didn't stop Matthew from staying to dinner that evening.

> Namioka, L. *Yang the Youngest and His Terrible Ear.*
> 1992, p. 49.

We looked at each other, but neither of us said anything. When you are close to someone, words are slippery things that slide away from what you want to say.

> Whelan, G. *Night of the Full Moon.* 1993, p. 40.

"Friends will take care of them," Mama said gently. "That's what friends do."

> Lowry, L. *Number the Stars.* 1991, p. 24.

Losing a best friend is one of the worst things that can happen to you.

> Hansen, J. *Yellow Bird and Me.* 1986, p. 6.

The teenager . . . was uncomfortable among her new classmates . . . . Even though the majority of them spoke Spanish and came from Cuba, Argentina, and Costa Rica, they were not like any of her friends back home.

> Gonzales, G. "Viva New Jersey." in Gallo, Donald R., ed.
> *Join In, Multiethnic Short Stories.* 1993, p. 52.

Initiating Experiences

The following suggestions are intended to use with students to initiate the theme study. They are designed to help students to relate to the theme, to activate their prior knowledge, and to arouse their interest in it. To help students become involved with their reading, we suggest varied types of experiences, oral activities or discussions, and writing experiences. These activities are related to the initiating stage of the Reader Involvement Model. While some of the activities may include more than one of these types, each will be categorized according to the emphasis of student activity.

- In a small group or as a class, brainstorm all the ways people can be alike or different.

- Select someone you know or have read about or have heard about that you would like to have as a friend. Explain why.

- With a classmate create a bumper sticker or poster about friendship.

- Create a recipe for friendship.

Response Log

Describe yourself as a friend. What characteristics do you bring to a friendship?

Response Log

Write a definition of friendship. What characteristics do you think a friend should have? After you have read some of the stories about people who are friends, reread and revise your original definition of friendship and list of characteristics.

Reading and Connecting Experiences

Picture Book

Picture books that relate diversity and friendship can be used effectively with older students to introduce them to a topic or to initiate class discussion.

Polacco, Patricia. *Chicken Sunday*. Philomel Books, 1992.

Three children in a diverse neighborhood want to buy a special Easter bonnet for their good friend, Miss Eula, but they do not have enough money. Unfairly accused of throwing eggs at Mr. Kodinski's store, they find a way to earn money for the hat while changing Mr. Kodinski's opinion of them. The colorful illustrations enhance this wonderful story of friendships among people of different ages, religions, and ethnic backgrounds.
Help your students to see how the illustrations enhance this text by showing the emotions of the characters in a way that words cannot express.

Responding Activities. See page 128.

OTHER PICTURE BOOKS

Fox, Mem. Illustrated by Julie Vivas. *Wilfrid Gordon McDonald Partridge.*

Polacco, Patricia. *Chicken Sunday.*

———. *Mrs. Katz and Tush.*

Focus Books

Focus books are ones in which the theme of a multifaceted view of friends and relationships is a central one to the book. These are books that have broad appeal and might be read and enjoyed by most students. We recommend that you select one or more of these titles for large group or whole class study.

Creech, Sharon. *Walk Two Moons*. HarperCollins, 1994. 280 pages.

In the 1995 Newbery Medal-winning book, Sal and her grandparents go to Idaho on an odyssey to find her mother. Sal is interested in reflecting on her American Indian heritage, too. But this is also a story within a story. Sal and her father have moved to town when they find out that her mother will not be coming home. Sal makes friends with Phoebe and Ben who help her deal with her loneliness. Ben lives with his aunt and uncle. Phoebe's mother goes away after leaving only notes for her family. Phoebe is overly imaginative and when her mother leaves, Phoebe creates fantastic stories to explain what has happened. Sal tells her grandparents Phoebe's story as they travel west, but she is really trying to understand her situation.
Sal is the narrator of this book. Help students to see how she comes to life through the stories that she tells of her experiences and of Phoebe's. Students also will find the technique of storytelling within the novel as an interesting way to reveal the complexity of the plot.

Responding Activities. See page 129.

Gonzales, Gloria. "Viva New Jersey." in Gallo, Donald R., ed. *Join In, Multiethnic Short Stories.* Delacorte Press, 1993. pp. 51-61.

Lucinda and her family escaped in a makeshift boat from Cuba and are now living in an apartment building in New Jersey. Lonely for her homeland and her grandmother, she feels uncomfortable and out-of-place in high school. She is led to develop a friendship with a girl who lives nearby after she befriends an abandoned dog who has created an emergency in her apartment building.

Before reading this short story with your students, provide them with information about why families fled from Cuba. Help them to identify with Lucinda's feelings. Have them consider what they might have done in a similar situation.

Responding Activities. See page 130.

Gordon, Shelia. *Waiting for the Rain.* Bantam, 1987. 214 pages.

Tengo is an African and Frikkie is white; Tengo's family works for a wealthy farmer and Frikkie is the farmer's nephew and heir. The boys have played together every vacation that Frikkie visits the farm, but as they grow older, the bond of childhood friendship is all that is left between them. Frikkie will inherit the land and without an education, Tengo would be fated to work for him. But that is not enough for Tengo. He goes to live with relatives and get an education. There is unrest in the township after Tengo has been there for three years. The white army comes in to quell the disturbance and Tengo and Frikkie are reunited for one more time, but they are on opposite sides.

This is a powerful book that students can read on many levels. Activating or developing your students' prior knowledge about apartheid and the conditions in South Africa will enhance their understanding of it. Class discussion as students read this book will also help them to clarify any misunderstandings and to develop deeper levels of understandings. This book frequently leads students to serious discussions about the personal tragedies caused by racial inequities and the larger societal implications.

Responding Activities. See page 131.

Hansen, Joyce. *Yellow Bird and Me.* Clarion Books, 1986. 155 pages.

Doris is lonely for her friend, Amir, who has moved away. Sixth grade without him is not the same especially since Yellow Bird, the class clown, is always bugging her to help him with his reading problem. As she grudgingly works with him, she begins to understand and care about him. Meanwhile, she tries to find a way to visit Amir and to cope with the strictness of her family. Amir's letters help her to see beyond Yellow Bird's silliness and to develop a new friendship with him as well.

This book will help youngsters to understand the difficulties faced by students with serious reading problems and to empathize with their embarrassment. It also can help them to explore the many different dimensions of friendship. Your class may also enjoy reading Hansen's *The Gift-Giver*, which precedes *Yellow Bird and Me.*

Responding Activities. See page 132.

Lowry, Lois. *Number the Stars*. Houghton Mifflin, 1989; Dell Yearling, 1990. 137 pages.

A 1990 Newbery Award Medal Winner, this story is set in Denmark in 1943 and tells how Annemarie Johansen and her family help her best friend, Ellen Rosen, and her family to escape from the Nazis. Copenhagen is a city under siege with the invading Nazis on every corner. Life has remained relatively normal for the best friends, ten year old Annemarie Johansen and Ellen Rosen, but they are frightened by the soldiers and they miss butter and other foods that are in short supply. They are proud of King Christian X who remains strong, even with Nazis in his country. Their normal life ends when the Nazis begin their "relocation" program for the Jews in Denmark. Annemarie's family does not sit idly by. They help Ellen's parents escape to the country and take Ellen in as their "third daughter." But the challenges for Annemarie are just beginning because she and her family must help reunite Ellen with her parents and then help them to escape to neutral Sweden.

Have students focus on the friendship between the two girls. Help them to discuss whether their acts of courage are believeable or not and why.

Responding Activities. See page 133.

Pitts, Paul. *Crossroads*. Avon Books, 1994. 152 pages.

When his mother inherited a rundown hotel in town, Hobart moved from the reservation. Living in the hotel with his mother and his old Uncle Tully, Hobart is lonely. He is slow to make friends at his new school and the class bully, Calvin, is always making fun of him. Everything changes when a family passing through town is stranded by car trouble and they stay at the hotel. Their daughter, Lettie Mendoza, is Hobart's age and she goes to school with him. Lettie makes friends quickly and helps Hobart to gain confidence and to stand up against Calvin.

The book includes a glossary with Navajo words, Spanish words, and Hobart's dictionary. Have students recognize how Pitts uses language to add to the story's effectiveness.

Responding Activities. See page 134.

Soto, Gary. *Pacific Crossing*. Harcourt Brace Jovanovich, 1992. 135 pages.

Pacific Crossing is the story of two friendships. The first is the life-long friendship between Lincoln Mendoza and his best friend, Tony Contreras. They have been studying martial arts when their school is asked to participate in a summer exchange program with a school in Japan. The principal taps the two of them for the program because of what they have learned in their martial arts classes. The exchange program sends the boys to stay with Japanese families for the summer. The second friendship is the one that develops between Lincoln and his Japanese host, Mitsuo. During his stay they share Japanese culture with him, and he shares American and Mexican American culture with Mitsuo's family.

This book can help students to learn about and value three cultures through the eyes of the main characters. As your students read, have them look for similarities and differences among the three cultures. Students can also discuss how people from different cultures become friends.

Responding Activities. See page 135.

Response Log:
Chicken Sunday

Talk to several adults you know asking them to describe family customs, traditions, or foods that have a special meaning to them. These might be related to holidays or religious observances. Use this information to make a collage.

Response Log:
Walk Two Moons

In small groups prepare a travelogue tracing the journey that Sal takes with her grandparents. Find information and pictures of those places that they visit.

Exploring Diversity. © 1996. Teacher Ideas Press. (800) 237-6124.

Response Log:
"Viva New Jersey"

"Viva New Jersey" is a short story. Imagine that it is the first chapter in a novel.

Write the next chapter in which Lucinda and Ashley have a misunderstanding based on their different family backgrounds. Use the fiction map to help you plan the chapter.

Plot:

Major Characters:

Conflict:

Resolution:

Climax:

Theme:

Exploring Diversity. © 1996. Teacher Ideas Press. (800) 237-6124.

Response Log:
Waiting for the Rain

The political situation in the South Africa where Frikkie and Tengo lived put constraints on their friendship. The following quotation illustrates when the division between the two became obvious, at least to Tengo. Write a paragraph, imagining that you are Tengo and express what you are thinking and then repeat the process, imagining that you are Frikkie. Be prepared to explain the differences between the boys.

"The oubaas is getting old," Tengo observed.

"When he dies," Frikkie said, "this whole farm will be mine. You can work for me and be my boss-boy."

Tengo picked up a heavy, flat, gray pebble from the riverbank, took aim at a tree stump on the opposite side, took a step back, and with an overarm swing threw the stone, hitting the tree stump dead center.

"Good shot," Frikkie said. He picked up a stone, aimed, threw, and missed. He sat down, learning against the trunk of a willow, pulled a straw of dry grass, and chewed on it. "Will you, Tengo?"

"Will I what?"

"Will you be my boss-boy when this is my farm?"

Tengo, with perfect aim, hit the tree stump with a second stone. He stood for a few moments, looking down at Frikkie's hair, which was the same yellow as the willow branches, then turned and walked off. (pp. 41-42)

Response Log:
Yellow Bird and Me

The relationships among the characters in *Yellow Bird and Me* are significant to understanding the story. Use the relationship chart to help you recognize how each gets along at school, with family, and with friends.

	School	Family	Friends
Doris			
Yellow Bird			
Amir			

Response Log:
Number the Stars

After reading *Number the Stars*, choose either Annemarie or Ellen and put yourself in her place in each of the following situations:

1. On the street with the Nazi soldiers.

2. When the Nazi soldiers come to the Johansen's apartment.

3. At the farmhouse the night the Rosens leave.

Plan to dramatize these events.

Response Log:
Crossroads

Relate an experience that you have had, read, or observed when a bully was causing trouble. How was the bully dealt with? How might it have been handled differently?

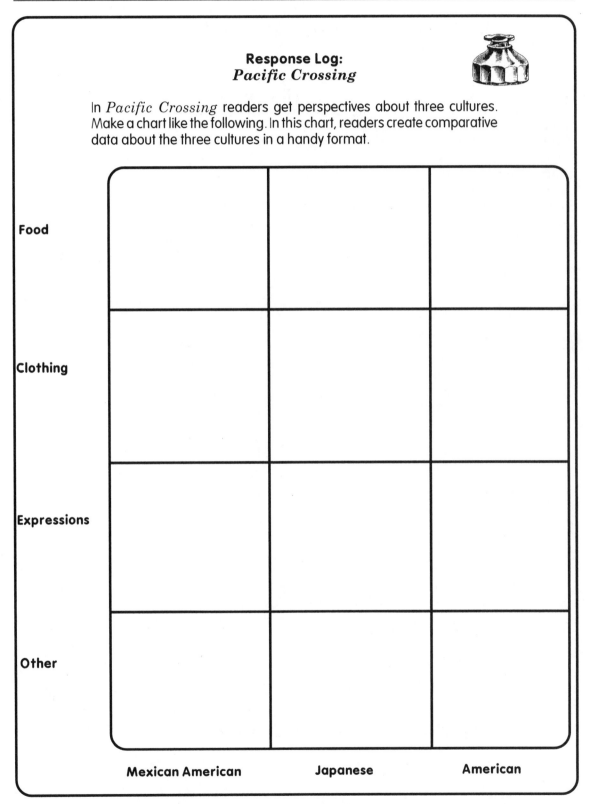

Response Log:
Pacific Crossing

In *Pacific Crossing* readers get perspectives about three cultures. Make a chart like the following. In this chart, readers create comparative data about the three cultures in a handy format.

	Mexican American	Japanese	American
Food			
Clothing			
Expressions			
Other			

Exploring Diversity. © 1996. Teacher Ideas Press. (800) 237-6124.

Reflecting and Internalizing Experiences

In this section, we have selected activities to help students respond to and reflect upon books that they have read or that they will read. The activities are designed to be general enough so that they can be applied to a number of different books rather than used with only a specific one. These activities can also be modified and adapted to be applied to specific books.

Use the following suggestions with students to aid them in responding to the books they are reading or to help students to reflect upon the theme and to extend their understanding of it. These experiences are varied, including oral activities or discussions, either small group or whole class; writing experiences in Reflection Logs; and exploration or creative activities, either small group or individual. These activities are designed to help students to internalize their reading and are related to the internalizing stage of the Reader Involvement Model. While some of the activities may include more than one of these types, each will be categorized according to the emphasis of student activity.

- Discuss which character from the stories you have read you would most like to have as a friend. Why?

- Scintillating Sentences: As you read, find a sentence that appeals to you. Record the sentence, with title, author, and page number, on strips of paper or chart paper and display in the classroom, along with your classmates' sentences. Compare and discuss the sentences. Write about why your sentence is significant to you. Also, you may want to use it as a springboard for doing more writing.

- "Nominate" some of the characters you have been reading about for awards that reveal something about them. For example:

  The award for the person who I would most want for a friend:

  Annemarie (*Number the Stars* by Lois Lowry)

  Explain your choices for the awards. In a group you may want to create new award categories and then make the nominations together. Page 137 provides a format for certificates for the characters. It is followed by a completed certificate and a sample for reproduction. Artwork can be added to the certificates. The artwork should complement the wording of the award. (Brown and Stephens, 1995, p. 64)

- Select a character whom you have found to be unforgettable. Work individually to clarify your own understanding of the character. Then join with another person who has selected a different character. Each of you assume the role of your character and introduce yourselves. Finally, prepare a ten-minute interaction between the two characters to present to the class.

Responding Activity:

Format for award certificates:

In recognition of

_____

(fill in character's name)

as or for

_____

(according to the award)

_____

(fill in the name of the award)

for contributions to

_____

(fill in book's title)

_____

Date   Signature

- Write about the following:

  One character I really liked was . . .

  One character I really disliked was . . .

  When I was reading, I thought about . . .

  The part that I liked best about the book (story/poem) was . . .

  The part that I liked least about the book (story/poem) was . . .

- Use the Interaction Chart to determine how characters demonstrate friendship. Select a character from a book you have read. On the chart, list the character, interaction with other key characters, and insights about friendship from these interactions. This will help you learn to respond critically and with empathy to the character.

Responding Activity:

Interaction Chart

Character	Interaction	Insights

- Character mapping is a useful tool to help you learn to understand the process of characterization in literature. In this process, you identify the character in a box in the middle of your paper. Then identify characteristics and qualities of that character and list each one individually in circles around the original box. Attach these new circles to each characteristic with lines leading back to the original circle. (See Responding Activity on page 140.)

  Next find support or evidence for the characteristics from your reading. The evidence or support is placed in other shapes around the appropriate characteristic with lines going back to it. Remember that the evidence may be found in a number of ways: the character's speech, actions, behaviors; other character's descriptions or comments; events; commentary from the narrator; illustrations; or the evidence may be inferred rather than directly stated. The evidence may also demonstrate more than one characteristic; therefore, it may have more than one line leading to more than one characteristic. Once you have completed your map, write about what you have graphically represented.

- Design a poster advertising the qualities of one of the characters you read about as a friend.

- In this activity, you will identify with and gain insight into characters by trading places with them. First, write about a memorable event in your life, such as a challenge you have faced, an embarrassing moment, or a frightening experience. Next, select a character that you like from your reading and identify the characteristics you admire. Then imagine that the character had your experience and act out how the character would respond to it.

- Find several songs about friendship and research their history. How are they representative of the times in which they were written?

CONNECTIONS ACROSS THE CURRICULUM

Students can increase their depth and breadth of understanding when they have opportunities to make connections among various content areas. The following suggestions are designed to help students relate this theme across the curriculum.

Social Studies

- Conflicts and wars between countries or states are frequently based on distrust and misunderstanding of other people's cultures. Friendships can help to build trust and understanding. Research historical situations in which distrust and misunderstandings between people of different cultures resulted in conflict or war.

- Research organizations that try to promote friendships among people of different cultures.

- Compare the situation in Gordon's *Waiting for the Rain* with South Africa today. How have things changed?

Responding Activity:
Character Mapping Experience

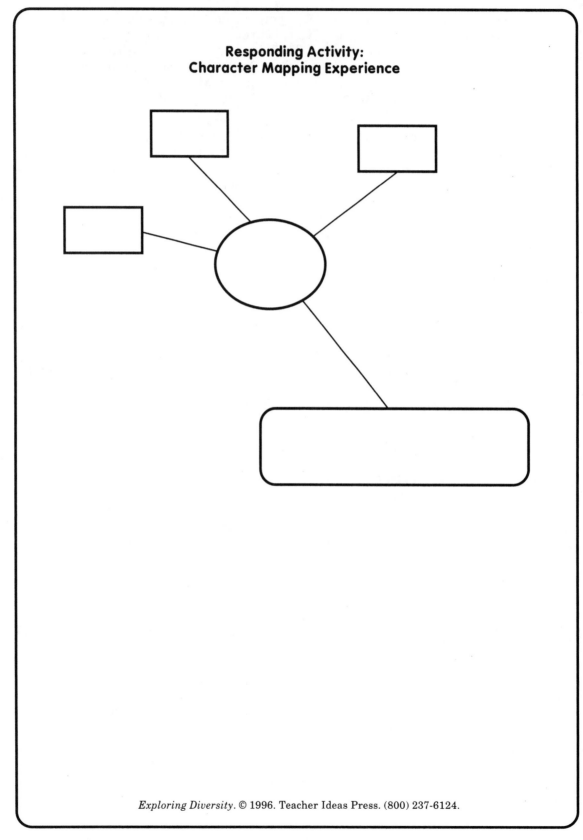

Response Log

It is always difficult to move to a new place and have to make new friends, but when you are the only person whose ethnic background is different from the rest of the students, it is frequently even more difficult. In your journal, write a journal entry, assuming the role of this new student in school. Write about how it feels and how you would handle the situation.

Science and Math

- Research scientific breakthroughs, inventions, and medical advances that benefited from or were the result of collaboration between people from one or more different cultures or countries.

Geography

- Natural boundaries can help or hinder the development of friendships among people from different countries. Examine an atlas to provide examples.

Physical Education

- How can sports and athletic events contribute to the development of friendships across cultures and between countries?

- Sports opened the door for Lincoln and Tony to go to Japan in Soto's *Pacific Crossing.* Discuss how competition can help to promote friendship among people of different cultures.

Further Reading

These titles relate to the theme of this chapter and could be used for whole class, small group, or individual reading.

Across Cultures

Bode, Janet. *New Kids in Town, Oral Histories of Immigrant Teens.*

Wolff, Virginia Euwer. *Make Lemonade.*

African American

Greenfield, Eloise. *Koya DeLaney and the Good Girl Blues.*

Guy, Rosa. *The Friends.*

Hansen, Joyce. *The Gift-Giver.*

———. *Home Boy.*

———. *Yellow Bird and Me.*

Myers, Walter Dean. *Fast Sam, Cool Clyde, and Stuff.*

———. *Hoops.*

———. *Motown and Didi.*

———. *The Outside Shot.*

———. *Won't Know Till I Get There.*

Taylor, Mildred. *The Friendship.*

Asia

Coerr, Eleanor. *Sadako and the Thousand Paper Cranes.*

Asian American

Namioka, Lensey. *Yang the Youngest and His Terrible Ear.*

Caribbean Islands

Taylor, Theodore. *The Cay.*

———. *Timothy of the Cay, A Prequel-Sequel.*

European American

Bauer, Marion Dane. *A Taste of Smoke.*

———. *On My Honor.*

Bridgers, Sue Ellen. *Keeping Christina.*

Cole, Brock. *The Goats.*

Crutcher, Chris. *Staying Fat for Sarah Byrnes.*

———. *Stotan.*

Fenner, Carol. *Randall's Wall.*

Hahn, Mary Downing. *Stepping on the Cracks.*

Hobbs, Will. *Downriver.*

Naylor, Phyllis Reynolds. *Reluctantly Alice.*

Peck, Richard. *Princess Ashley.*

———. *Remembering the Good Times.*

European Immigrant

Nixon, Joan Lowery. *Land of Hope.*

Holocaust

Lowry, Lois. *Number the Stars.*

Orgel, Doris. *The Devil in Vienna.*

Orlev, Uri. Translated from the Hebrew by Hillel Halkin. *The Man from the Other Side.*

Richter, Hans Peter. Translated from the German by Edite Kroll. *Friedrich.*

Jewish

Levoy, Myron. *Alan and Naomi.*

Semel, Nava. Translated by Semour Simckes. *Becoming Gershona.*

Mexican American

Soto, Gary. *Taking Sides.*

Native American

Dowd, John. *Ring of Tall Trees.*

Pitts, Paul. *The Shadowman's Way.*

Speare, Elizabeth George. *The Sign of the Beaver.*

Whelan, Gloria. *Night of the Full Moon.*

Turkey

Hiçyilmaz, Gaye. *Against the Storm.*

Collections

Bolden, Tonya, ed. *Rites of Passage, Stories About Growing up by Black Writers from Around the World.*

Carlson, Lori M., and Cynthia L. Ventura, eds. *Where Angels Glide at Dawn, New Stories from Latin America.*

Gallo, Donald R., ed. *Join In, Multiethnic Short Stories.*

Mazer, Anne, ed. *America Street, A Multicultural Anthology of Stories.*

Nye, Naomi Shihab, selected by. *This Same Sky, A Collection of Poems from Around the World.*

Pettepiece, Thomas, and Anatoly Aleksin, eds. *Face to Face, A Collection of Stories by Celebrated Soviet and American Writers.*

Rochman, Hazel, selected by. *Somehow Tenderness Survives, Stories of Southern Africa.*

Soto, Gary. *A Fire in My Hands, A Book of Poems.*

Strickland, Michael R., selected by. Illustrated by Alan Leiner. *Poems That Sing to You.*

Thomas, Joyce Carol, ed. *A Gathering of Flowers, Stories About Being Young in America.*

Wilson, Budge. *The Leaving and Other Stories.*

8

Celebrating Diversity
Books and Authors Too Good to Miss

Teachers are always finding books that are so good that they capture students' interest and encourage them to keep reading. These are the books that students say they cannot put down. We know that when students discover a book they enjoy, they become unofficial press agents for it. Students urge their friends to read the books that they enjoy and often pass tattered copies of well-liked books back and forth among themselves. Students also frequently find an author that they like and then read everything written by that person.

In this chapter we identify books and authors too good to miss. The books we describe have received critical acclaim or awards and are well received by students. The authors we present are recognized as significant contributors to the field or are promising new writers. These are authors that young people want to read. The books and authors in this chapter have a broad appeal for all young people from a variety of ethnic and cultural backgrounds.

Books Too Good to Miss

While there are many excellent books to use to celebrate diversity, we have selected eight picture books and twelve novels that we believe make an excellent contribution.

Picture Books

Bruchac, Joseph. *Fox Song*. Illustrated by Paul Morin. New York: Philomel Books, a division of Putnam & Grosset Group, 1993.

Grama Bowman shared her Abenaki Indian heritage with Jamie, her great-granddaughter. She spent a lot of time with Jamie and told her stories of their people and of the woods where they walked together. When Grama Bowman was no longer there, Jamie was sad. But as she went into the woods and sang the song that Grama taught her, Jamie knew that she would never be alone.

Responding Activities. See page 148.

Bruchac, Joseph, and Jonathan London. *Thirteen Moons on Turtle's Back*. Illustrated by Thomas Locker. New York: Philomel Books, 1992.

The turtle's shell has thirteen scales on its back, one for each of the thirteen moons of the year. The authors select Native American legends to explain the year of the moons. Each of the moons has its own name and a story to go with it. This collection includes a poem and a painting about each of the moons that captures a sense of the Native American connection with the land.

Responding Activities. See page 149.

Bunting, Eve. *A Day's Work*. New York: Clarion Books, 1994.

Francisco's grandfather speaks only Spanish, so he goes with his grandfather, his abuelo, to find work. Francisco tells a prospective employer that his grandfather is an experienced gardener in order to get him a day's work. But his grandfather knew nothing of gardening. His task is to weed a banking and so Francisco and his grandfather begin pulling out all the plants and leaving the flowers. When their boss returns he is shocked to see that all of his plants have been uprooted and the flowers (chickweed) remain. The grandfather teaches Francisco a lesson as he makes amends for his mistake.

Responding Activities. See page 150.

Bunting, Eve. *Smoky Night*. Illustrated by David Diaz. San Diego: Harcourt Brace Jovanovich, 1994.

During the Los Angeles riots, Daniel and his mother watch the looting from their darkened apartment. They are later awakened as smoke fills their apartment building. The people from the neighborhood are taken to safety in a shelter, but Daniel can't find his cat. Their neighbor, Mrs. Kim, must also go to the shelter. Her cat and Daniel's always have fought, but now they are both missing. The cats are found, hiding together. They provide a lesson for their owners about getting along in this 1995 Caldecott Medal winner.

Responding Activities. See page 151.

Heide, Florence Parry and Judith Heide Gulliland. *Sami and the Time of the Troubles*. Illustrated by Ted Lewin. New York: Clarion Books, 1992.

Sami, age 10, is growing up in a battle zone in Beirut, Lebanon. When there is fighting going on around them, he and his family have to live in his uncle's basement where they will be safe from the gun fire. But there are also quiet days when the fighting ceases and Sami and the other residents of Beirut have the freedom to go outside. The memories of the quiet times and the family's experiences have to sustain them during the time of the troubles.

Responding Activities. See page 152.

McKissack, Patricia C., and Fredrick L. McKissack. *Christmas in the Big House, Christmas in the Quarters*. Illustrated by John Thompson. New York: Scholastic, 1994.

In this Coretta Scott King Award winning book, the McKissacks present life on a Virginia plantation at Christmas in 1859. They present the traditions and customs of both the wealthy plantation owners and the slaves who live on the plantation. The book includes songs, recipes, and details of what life would be like for everyone living on the plantation.

Responding Activities. See page 153.

Mora, Pat. *Listen to the Desert Oye al Desierto*. Illustrated by Francisco X. Mora. New York: Clarion Books, 1994.

This book presents the images and sounds of the southwestern desert. Each page has the sounds of nature, the animals and the weather, in both English and Spanish.

Responding Activities. See page 154.

Stanley, Fay. *The Last Princess: The Story of Princess Ka'iulani of Hawaii*. Illustrated by Diane Stanley. New York: Four Winds Press, 1991.

Princess Ka'iulani was the next in line to assume the throne of Hawaii. She was away from the islands in England, preparing to be a well-educated monarch for the island. The white families living on the islands were becoming increasingly powerful and wished to have the United States annex Hawaii. Princess Ka'iulani left England and traveled to the United States to meet with President Grover Cleveland to request that he honor the opposition of the Hawaiian people to annexation. President Cleveland honored a commitment not to annex the islands; however, he was unwilling to oppose the white people who were effectively ruling the islands. The Hawaiians tried a revolt to take back their islands, but their efforts failed. The monarchy of Hawaii was over; Princess Ka'iulani would never rule her country.

Responding Activities. See page 155.

Response Log:
Fox Song

Think about an older person who has been an influence in your life.
Write about a special memory about your relationship.

Response Log:
Thirteen Moons on Turtle's Back

Create your own calendar. Name and describe the months according to a description of the time that you think captures a feeling of time.

Response Log:
A Day's Work

In this story, a potentially difficult situation turns out to be a good lesson for Francisco. Describe a situation that you have experienced or observed in which you learned an important lesson.

Response Log:
Smoky Night

In this book the cats serve as a way for people to learn to communicate with one another. Cite an example, either from your experiences or from your reading, where a pet helped people make connections.

Response Log:
Sami and the Time of the Troubles

Imagine that you live in a war zone. You have spent weeks without being able to go outside, to see your friends, or even to go to school. Then there is a cease fire. Describe how you would spend your first day back out in the world.

Response Log:
Christmas in the Big House,
Christmas in the Quarters

Talk with members of your family and create your own description
of customs and traditions the family has observed over the years.

Response Log:
Listen to the Desert Oye al Desierto

Imagine that you are traveling in a desert. Describe, using as many of your senses as possible, your experiences.

Response Log:
The Last Princess: The Story of
Princess Ka'iulani of Hawaii

Speculate about what would have happened if the Hawaiian people had been able to maintain the monarchy. How would that have affected Hawaii's statehood? What would it be like if it still had a king or queen?

Twelve Novels Too Good to Miss

Bauer, Joan. *Thwonk*. New York: Delacorte, 1995. 215 pages.

A. J., a high school senior, has talent and a dream, but she also has a problem. Herein is the basis for the conflict of this humorous novel. She is a gifted photographer; her dream is to pursue her talent and attend a good art school to study photography and prepare for a career; and her problem is that she is in love with Peter, but he does not know she is alive.

As she searches for the right image for the cover of the Valentine's issue of the school paper, she finds a cupid doll. The cupid comes alive and offers A. J. the choice of receiving his help in one aspect of her life: artistically, academically, or romantically. A. J. chooses help in having Peter fall in love with her, but she got more than she bargained for when he becomes totally devoted to her. This complication adds to the conflict she is experiencing with her father as he opposes her going to art school and seeking a career in photography.

Responding Activities. See page 160.

Choi, Sook Nyul. *Year of Impossible Goodbyes*. New York: Dell Yearling, 1991. 169 pages.
———. *Echoes of the White Giraffe*. Boston: Houghton Mifflin, 1993. 137 pages.

Choi presents a vivid picture of life in Korea from the closing days of World War II to the years directly following the Korean War in her books, *Year of Impossible Goodbyes* and its sequel, *Echoes of the White Giraffe*. In the first book, she describes the last months of the thirty-five year Japanese occupation. Sookan, her mother, and younger brother are separated from her father and her older brothers in the Japanese occupied territory of northern Korea. The Japanese rule strictly and demand that the Koreans abandon their customs. Life is difficult for Sookan and her family, but when the war ends they have hope that the family will be reunited and that things will get back to normal. When the Japanese flee, however, they are replaced almost immediately by the Russians who initially appear to be more benevolent than the Japanese. Their benevolence lasts only until they have a strong enough hold to begin their communist indoctrination program. Sookan and her family decide that they must flee from the Russian occupied north to the south where American troops are protecting the territory. In the sequel, war has again disrupted the family's life. Sookan, her mother, and brother are forced to flee their home in Seoul. She spends much of her adolescence living in the refugee housing in the hills of Pusan where she learns about herself, love, and holding on to her dreams.

Responding Activities. See page 161.

Conly, Jane Leslie. *Crazy Lady*. New York: HarperCollins, 1993. 180 pages.

After his mother's death things do not go well for Vernon. He is lonely; he is not doing well in school; and he realizes that his dream to play baseball for the Baltimore Orioles will never be fulfilled. But Vernon is resourceful. He finds a retired teacher, Miss Annie, who lives in the neighborhood to tutor him, and she also becomes his friend. Instead of payment for the tutoring, Vernon is to help around Miss Annie's house. She also has him help her friend Maxine. Maxine, the Crazy Lady, is the neighborhood outcast, a drunk who yells at neighbor kids who in turn taunt her and her son Ronald, who is retarded. Vernon learns a great deal about life from Miss Annie, but he also learns from Maxine and from Ronald.

Responding Activities. See page 162.

Dorris, Michael. *Morning Girl*. New York: Hyperion Books, 1992. 74 pages.

Morning Girl might be called the last day of innocence as it tells of the Taino family living in accord and harmony with nature on their Bahamian island. It is the simple story of Morning Girl's life. As their names imply, she and her brother, Star Boy, are as different from one another as they can be. They tell of their life, narrating alternate chapters. Morning Girl is up with the sun enjoying the wonders of the day, while Star Boy sleeps through the day and explores after dark. Their life is simple and happy.

Morning Girl sees visitors approaching the island in their strangely squared canoe. Visitors are to be welcomed so she swims out to greet them. She is amused by their strange manner of dressing and by the language they speak, which she does not understand. Morning Girl returns to shore to summon her parents who will greet the guests officially. The year is 1492.

Responding Activities. See page 163.

McColley, Kevin. *The Walls of Pedro Garcia*. New York: Delacorte Press, 1993. 100 pages.

Pedro Garcia never had a childhood. He worked in the fields alongside his grandfather until he was old enough to work on his own. At twelve he considers himself to be grown up and feels that he must play the role of a man. He and his grandfather live and work on the estate of a wealthy Mexican family. From their hut Pedro and his grandfather can look down on the river and its breezes cool them and clear away the odors from the huts. Pedro feels a sense of competition with the head groundskeeper, Señor Warden, an American. He is in charge of the grounds and the workers and makes decisions that anger and frustrate Pedro. When Warden supervises the building of a high wall around the estate, the workers are all disturbed. The wall blocks the view of the river and traps the odors from the huts, making life unpleasant. For Pedro, the wall presents an opportunity to question Warden and to challenge him by going to the owner to complain.

Responding Activities. See page 164.

Matas, Carol. *Sworn Enemies*. New York: Dell Publishing, 1993. 132 pages.

For the twenty-nine years between 1827 and 1856, the Tsar's policy of forced conscription allows boys as young as twelve to be drafted for twenty-five year military service. Because of the heavy demands on the Jewish community, captors (khappers) were chosen by Jewish authorities to meet the quotas. In this book, the systematic discrimination against Jews by Tsar Nicholas is exemplified by the relationship between two young Jewish boys. Aaron is a yeshiva student who is valued by his community, while Zev is a khapper. As a promising scholar, Aaron is protected from military service by his community. Zev dislikes and resents Aaron for his station in the community and because he is betrothed to Miriam. When he is one "recruit" short of his quota, Zev kidnaps Aaron. For betraying the wishes of the community, Zev has to flee to another town. He, in turn, is kidnapped for the military where he and Aaron meet again and their survival becomes intertwined although they are bitter enemies.

Responding Activities. See page 165.

Qualey, Marsha. *Revolutions of the Heart*. Boston: Houghton Mifflin Company, 1993. 184 pages.

Other than being grounded for another in a series of automobile accidents, Cory Knutson seems to have everything going for her. She is smart, popular, and gets along with everyone. But her life is about to take a number of significant turns and changes. Cory meets Mac at a powwow that she and her mother attend. He is a new transfer to her school and is a member of the local tribe. Cory likes Mac and she realizes that he is interested in her. Their romance short circuits before it begins when Cory's mother collapses and is hospitalized with a seriously deteriorating heart condition. Even after her mother returns home, she is an invalid awaiting a donor for a heart transplant. During her mother's illness, Cory just wants to stay close to home without the involvement of a new boyfriend, but she and Mac do become friends. Her small school has not experienced any inter-racial dating or even any social interaction between the white and the Native American students. As they begin to date, they encounter discrimination from other students, but for Cory her brother's opposition is the most painful.

Responding Activities. See page 166.

Staples, Suzanne Fisher. *Shabanu: Daughter of the Wind.* New York: Alfred A. Knopf, 1989. 240 pages.
———. *Haveli.* New York: Alfred A. Knopf, 1993. 259 pages.

Shabanu, a Newbery Honor Book, tells the story of a courageous and intelligent young girl in the Cholistan Desert in Pakistan. In a first person account, Shabanu relates her love of her life helping her father tend their camels. The second daughter in a loving nomadic family with no sons, Shabanu's strong-willed independence has enabled her to have freedoms unknown to most Muslim girls. Yet as she approaches puberty at age twelve, her parents become concerned that she follow the strict Islamic traditions of their culture. When they arrange a marriage for her, Shabanu contemplates running away. She struggles to resolve the conflict between upholding her family's honor and her fierce need and desire to be her own person. *Haveli*, the sequel to Shabanu, tells the story of Shabanu's life six years later. Now the fourth wife of a wealthy and powerful elderly clan leader, Shabanu tries to protect herself and her young daughter in the daily intrigues with the other wives, their children, and families. Conditions become increasingly dangerous and life-threatening. Shabanu must outwit her enemies and make difficult decisions affecting the rest of her life. While these books are far removed from the experiences of most American students, the stories are so compelling that the readers are able to share Shabanu's life and experience a different world.

Responding Activities. See page 167.

Taylor, Theodore. *The Cay.* New York: Avon Books, 1969. 144 pages.
———. *Timothy of the Cay, A Prequel-Sequel.* San Diego: Harcourt Brace Jovanovich, 1993. 161 pages.

The Cay, Taylor's powerful story of a prejudiced young white boy and a wise old West Indian man, has sold more than a million copies since it was written in 1969. Set in the Caribbean during World War II, the story is told in a first person narrative by Phillip, an eleven year old American boy who lives with his parents on an island off the coast of Venezuela, where his father works for an oil and gas refinery. Phillip's mother hates the islands and has taught Phillip to look down on its dark-skinned native inhabitants. Phillip and his mother are on a ship returning to the safety of the United States when the ship is torpedoed. Thrown from the ship, Phillip is adrift on a raft with Timothy, a member of the ship's crew, and the ship's cat when he discovers he is blind. They make their way to a cay, a tiny deserted and uncharted island. Phillip not only learns to overcome his prejudice against Timothy but grows to respect and love him, as they struggle to survive the life-threatening hardships of their ordeal. *Timothy of the Cay*, published in 1993, tells the life of Timothy as a young man in the prequel and the life of Phillip after his rescue from the cay in the sequel.

Responding Activities. See page 168.

Response Log:
Thwonk

What goals do you have for the future? How will you achieve these goals?

Response Log:
Year of Impossible Goodbyes

Tradition plays a major role in Korean life. Identify 5 examples of ways in which tradition ruled Sookan's life.

Response Log:
Crazy Lady

Maxine and Ronald are different. Because they are different, kids ridicule them. Briefly discuss why some people treat anyone who is different badly.

Response Log:
Morning Girl

Imagine that you are a member of Morning Girl's family. How would you try to communicate with the visitors? Role play the situation with class members taking the role of both the family and a delegation of visitors.

Response Log:
The Walls of Pedro Garcia

The dream that Pedro has about the deer plays a significant role in his life. Briefly explain its significance and how it is tied to his feeling of being a man.

Response Log:
Sworn Enemies

Aaron and Zev are enemies. How does Aaron keep from becoming like Zev?

Response Log:
Revolutions of the Heart

Think about the way that some people treated Cory and Mac. Relate your own observations or experiences and briefly discuss examples of discrimination that you have observed.

Response Log:
Shabanu: Daughter of the Wind

Shabanu was frequently in conflict with the customs and traditions of her culture. In what ways are some of the young people you know in conflict with the expectations of society? What are the tough decisions they face?

Response Log:
The Cay **and**
Timothy of the Cay, A Prequel-Sequel

Imagine that you are Phillip struggling to survive on the cay. Keep a journal for a week recording your daily experiences, thoughts, and feelings.

More Responding Activities

Book reports often end up being a summary of the book jacket. Alternatives to traditional book reports, whether oral or written, can promote student involvement with books. Numerous alternatives are available, but we will examine three ways of getting students to talk about their reading: literature circles, book talks, and book sharing. We will discuss these types of learning opportunities from the most structured to the least structured.

Literature Circles

Literature circles are a way of structuring small group work to help students focus on a book or books. These circles are composed of 3-5 students with the students reading individual books or the same book. The teacher provides direction to the circle about the aspect of the book that they should examine. For example, the concept of theme in a work might be the focal point of the literature circle. The teacher might structure the circles so that students will be reading books with similar themes. Or the focus might be on characterization. Students might be directed to compare and contract ways in which characters are developed in their books. Within this type of learning structure, the emphasis is on the students to explore and discover among themselves.

Book Talks

Students present a book that they have read to the class. A book talk should last no longer than 10 minutes maximum. There should be three clearly defined steps to book talks. First, students show their book, give the title, the author's name, and the illustrator's name (if applicable). Second, they summarize major events in the book leading up to the climax, do a character study of one or more characters, or focus on a particular aspect of the book. They tell just enough to encourage others to read the book. Finally, they give their recommendation about the book.

Book Sharing

Book sharing is the most informal of these approaches. As the name implies, book sharing is simply giving students the opportunity to recommend a book that they have recently read and enjoyed (or have not liked at all). Book sharing should be brief snapshots about books. It should provide others with just enough information to know if they might like to read the book or not. Book sharing is fueled by students' enthusiasm about their reading. Teachers can provide a few minutes at the beginning of class several times a week or a longer time once a week for book sharing.

Authors Too Good to Miss

While there are numerous excellent writers who provide young readers with a broadened multicultural perspective, we have selected six authors to describe in this chapter. We used the following criteria for selecting them: a significant and varied body of work, well-developed characters, effectively structured plots, and meaningful themes. These authors present a vital and vivid picture of their heritage and their works make a contribution to a cultural awareness for their readers.

Marion Dane Bauer

Marion Dane Bauer writes compelling stories, marked by their intensity and economy of language. A full-time writer, she lives in Minnesota where she also teaches writing to aspiring adult writers. Her books have received numerous awards including the Newbery Honor Book Award for *On My Honor* and the Jane Addam Peace Award for *Rain of Fire.*

Marion Dane Bauer describes her seventh and eighth grade years as "absolutely horrendous." Many of her books reflect the complex emotions she experienced as she was growing up. Transcending ethnic and racial differences, her characters, their conflicts, and feelings are those with which all young people can identify. Joel, in *On My Honor,* becomes caught up in bragging to his best friend and telling half-truths to his father with disastrous results. Michael, in *Face to Face,* fantasizes about his absent father, desperately wanting his love and approval. Caitlin, in *A Taste of Smoke,* is hurt when the older sister she adores pays more attention to a new boyfriend than to her. But Caitlin does not know how to express her feelings or how to handle them.

A frequent theme in Bauer's stories is the conflict between illusion and reality. In *Face to Face,* Michael suffers terrible disillusionment when he goes to live with his father and his father seems to be disappointed in him. Finally, Michael must accept that his father is not the person he has imagined him to be. In *On My Honor,* the boys' bravado in a dangerous river leads to the awful reality of a fatal swim. In *A Taste of Smoke,* Caitlin struggles to determine whether the young boy who keeps appearing to her in the woods is real or a ghost. In her recently published book, *A Question of Trust,* the sons must adjust to their mother leaving home. It deals with issues of divorce and honesty.

Marion Dane Bauer also writes nonfiction. Among her best known is *What's Your Story?* This book is a helpful guide for young people who are learning to write fiction.

Responding Activities. See page 174.

Joyce Hansen

Joyce Hansen, a former teacher and staff development specialist in the New York public schools, exemplifies the old principle of writing that says "write about what you know." She writes about the African American experience from three distinct perspectives all of which build on her gifts as a storyteller. She writes fiction from two perspectives, either realistic contemporary or historical. The third perspective is as the author of nonfiction, writing about the role of African Americans during and after the Civil War.

In the realistic novels, *The Gift Giver, Yellow Bird and Me,* and *Home Boy,* Joyce Hansen writes of the young people of the Bronx. She speaks of the young people of the neighborhood, for this is where she grew up and where she still teaches.

Her three historical novels, *Out from This Place, Which Way Freedom?* and *The Captive* share the common theme of slavery and its effects. Each of the books provides the characters with a release from slavery and presents them with the opportunities and challenges to make their freedom meaningful.

Accompanying her fictionalized historical accounts, Joyce Hansen has lent her storyteller voice to a nonfiction account of the role of African American soldiers during the Civil War in *Between 2 Fires.* Hansen, thus, provides her readers with a perspective that has not often been explored. She is currently completing another work of nonfiction. This book will relate the experiences of African Americans during Reconstruction.

Responding Activities. See pages 175 and 176.

Walter Dean Myers

Walter Dean Myers is a versatile writer of fiction and nonfiction for young people. Since the 1970s, his work has helped to redefine how African American young people and their experiences are portrayed in children's and young adult literature. Myers' work has received numerous awards and is praised for its authenticity and sensitive treatment of relevant themes. His work is also noteworthy for its humor, imagery, and dialogue.

Born in West Virginia, Walter Dean Myers, beginning at age three, was raised in Harlem by foster parents when his mother died and his father had difficulty caring for eight children. His foster parents, the Deans, became for him his "real" parents. His father, though barely able to read and write, and his grandfather were great storytellers. His mother taught him to read using *True Romance* magazines and *Classic Comics* when he was four years of age.

Myers' school years were a difficult time for him. Although he could read well and his test scores indicated he was bright, he was frequently in fights and other kinds of trouble as a result of the anger and frustration he felt when the children teased him about his speech problems. Along the way, several teachers had a significant influence on his development as a writer. His adolescent years were especially difficult and at seventeen he quit high school to join the army. Following his army years, he worked at a succession of jobs as he was tying to develop himself as a writer. Rudine Sims Bishop in Twayne's United States Authors Series, *Presenting Walter Dean Myers* (1991), has written an interesting and thorough biography of Myers with an insightful analysis of his work.

Responding Activities. See page 177.

Gary Soto

Gary Soto is both amazingly prolific and versatile. He writes short stories, poetry, and essays as well as fiction for young people. Soto often writes about being young in the Central Valley of California where he grew up in a Mexican American neighborhood. His story collections such as *Baseball in April, Living up the Street, Small Faces,* and *Local News* capture the simplicity of daily life while framing it in astute observations about human nature. Fresno is the setting for *The Pool Party* in which ten year old Rudy, from a working class family, is invited to the pool party of a wealthy classmate. Rudy bridges the social distance by arriving at the party with a huge inner tube. In his book *The Skirt,* Miata must "rescue" her mother's folklorica skirt, which she forgot on the school bus. She plans to wear it in the dance program and does not want her parents to think she is careless. When her parents surprise her with a new skirt of her own, she reflects upon traditions. In his two novels, *Taking Sides* and *Pacific Crossing,* the setting shifts to the San Francisco Bay area and to Japan. In *Taking Sides,* Soto relates the experiences of Lincoln Mendoza as he adjusts to a new school and confronts his old school on the basketball court. Issues of loyalty and sportsmanship arise for Lincoln. In its sequel, *Pacific Crossing,* Lincoln moves back to his old neighborhood and returns to his old school. His interest and experience in martial arts pays off when his principal selects him to travel to Japan where he spends a summer in a Japanese home as an exchange student. This book provides students with a view of three cultures. Soto's stories have a poetic quality to them that make the commonplace unique. Gary Soto now lives in Berkeley, where he teaches creative writing at the University of California.

Responding Activities. See page 178.

Virginia Euwer Wolff

Virginia Euwer Wolff teaches English at Mt. Hood Academy, a small private school in Oregon. Her experiences as a teacher are evident as she presents young people and the challenges that they face. While Virginia Wolff has not been writing as long as some other authors, we believe that it is appropriate to include her because each of her books presents a different facet of the diversity of our culture. Additionally, each of her books has received positive critical and popular acclaim. In her first book, *Probably Still Nick Swansen,* she creates a mildly learning disabled character who struggles to deal with his world. Wolff draws from her experiences as an accomplished violinist herself as she creates a sense of the intensity that it takes to be a gifted musician. Allegra, the main character of her second novel, *The Mozart Season,* is a gifted musical prodigy who is preparing for a major violin competition. She also becomes aware of her heritage when her paternal grandmother sends her a gift. The gift is a purse that her mother had given her daughter (Allegra's grandmother) when she was sent to the United States to escape the Nazis. Allegra's great-grandmother died in a Nazi concentration camp. Her most recent book, *Make Lemonade,* a Golden Kite Award winning book, gives voice to the vast number of American youth who live in poverty. Her powerful account presents children of poverty without designating them as members of any specific racial or ethnic group. Certainly poverty does cross over all lines. This book is the story of a remarkable young girl, LaVaughn, whose greatest goal is to go to college after high school. To make money she takes a job as baby-sitter for two young children whose single mother Jolly is struggling to survive. LaVaughn nurtures and encourages Jolly and her children and essentially creates a sense of family and well being for them.

Responding Activities. See page 179.

Laurence Yep

Laurence Yep is a prolific writer whose books have won many awards. He was raised by his Chinese American parents above their grocery store in an African American neighborhood in San Francisco. A full-time writer, Yep writes in several genres for young people, including historical fiction, realistic fiction, mysteries, science fiction, and folktales. He also writes for the theater.

As a kid, Laurence Yep always felt like an outsider. He went to school in Chinatown where he was one of only a few students who did not speak Chinese. His parents and brother were excellent athletes, but he was not very good in sports. He says that he writes to let young people know that it is all right to be different and that eventually they will find their peer group where they will be accepted and valued for what they do. Yep published his first story when he was a senior in high school, and then went on to earn a doctorate in American Literature.

Dragon's Gate is a good example of Laurence Yep's work. Set during the last half of the nineteenth century in China and the western United States, the historical basis for this captivating story is the building of the first transcontinental railroad with Chinese laborers. Otter is a young Chinese boy who is forced to flee his homeland. His dreams of vast riches and unlimited opportunities in America are shattered when he joins his father and uncle. Together they become a part of a group of Chinese immigrants who endure incredible hardships and unfair treatment to build the railroad. Yep's portrayal of Otter is an excellent example of strong character development. Otter's strengths and weaknesses are wholly believable and readers are able to identify with him. Yep also use imagery and symbolism effectively to tell this story.

Responding Activities. See page 180.

Response Log:
Marion Dane Bauer

Marion Dane Bauer's books often relate the stories of young people who are facing conflict and difficult choices. They experience uncomfortable feelings and must find a way to solve their problems. From your own experiences or those of someone else you know, create a story about a similar situation.

Response Log:
Joyce Hansen

Read a biography or autobiography of an African American who has made significant contributions to our nation, but is not well-known. Prepare a presentation to the class about this person. Be sure to use visuals in your presentation, also. Use the following adaptation of a newspaper format to plan your presentation. It also provides for your reaction and opinions. The format is as follows:

Who—a brief identification of the person

When—dates that the person lived

Where—significant places person lived and worked

What—major contributions or accomplishments

Significance—major importance of the contributions

Role Model—qualities to be emulated

Personal Reactions—your reactions to the person and book

Exploring Diversity. © 1996. Teacher Ideas Press. (800) 237-6124.

Presentation Notes

Who?

When?

Where?

What?

Significance?

Role Model?

Personal reactions?

Response Log:
Walter Dean Myers

Walter Dean Myers draws upon his own experiences as a child and adolescent to help him write books that connect with young people. Think of yourself as an author. Select one of your experiences as the basis for a story, but change it so that it has some new characters and events in it.

Response Log:
Gary Soto

Gary Soto's stories are "neighborhood" stories. Using one as a model, write a story about your own neighborhood.

Response Log:
Virginia Euwer Wolff

Virginia Euwer Wolff's books are about young people who are different from others in some significant ways, yet share many of the same needs and feelings as everyone else their age. Describe what you think these needs and feelings are.

Response Log:
Laurence Yep

Laurence Yep uses historical events as the basis for some of his books. Research a historical event that captures your interest. Create a story about someone your age who is involved in this event. With the help of some of your classmates, use Readers Theater to perform your story for the class.

Author Study

Responding Activity

If students are going to focus their reading on a single writer, even for a short period, they need to look at each title as part of a whole. They need to see the interrelationships of each title to the entire body of the author's works. The following figure (see page 182) provides a chart on which students can sketch out various literary aspects of each work. This chart is a useful way to begin to identify patterns and similarities among the works of an author as well as recognizing that a good author presents a uniqueness in each work.

Responding Activity: Author Study

Biographical Information

Title				
Plot				
Character				
Setting				
Conflicts				
Themes				

Celebrating Diversity with Award-Winning Books

The following information lists significant awards and the books recognized from 1989-1995.

JANE ADDAMS CHILDREN'S BOOK AWARD

Sponsored by the Women's International League for Peace and Freedom and the Jane Addams Peace Association. Begun in 1953 for the children's book of the year that has "themes stressing peace, social justice, world community and the equality of the sexes and all races."

1995 *Kids at Work: Lewis Hine and the Crusade Against Child Labor* by Russell Freedman.

1994 *Freedom's Children: Young Civil Rights Activists Tell Their Own Stories* by Ellen Levine.

1993 *A Taste of Salt: A Story of Modern Haiti* by Frances Temple.

1992 *Journey of the Sparrows* by Fran Buss.

1991 *Big Book for Peace* edited by Ann Durrell and Marilyn Sachs.

1990 *A Long Hard Journey: The Story of the Pullman Porter* by Patricia McKissack and Fredrick McKissack.

1989 (joint winners)

Anthony Burns: The Defeat & Triumph of a Fugitive Slave by Virginia Hamilton.

Looking Out by Victoria Boutis.

MILDRED L. BATCHELDER AWARD

This award is presented annually by the American Library Association. It is awarded to an outstanding children's book originally published in a foreign language in a foreign country, and then subsequently published in the United States.

1996 *The Lady with the Hat* by Uri Orlev.

1995 *The Boy from St. Petri* by Bjorne Reuter.

1993 *The Apprentice* by Pilar M. Llorente.

1992 *The Man from the Other Side* by Uri Orlev.

1991 *A Hand Full of Stars* by Rafik Schami.

1990 *Buster's World* by Bjarne Reuter.

1989 *Crutches* by Peter Hartling.

BOSTON GLOBE-HORN BOOK AWARD

The Boston Globe-Horn Book Award has been presented annually since 1967 by the Boston Globe and the Horn Book Magazine for outstanding text and outstanding illustration.

1995   Fiction: *Some of the Kinder Planets* by Tim Wynne-Jones.
        Honor Books: *Jericho* by Janet Hickman.
                   Earthshine by Theresa Nelson.
        Nonfiction: *Abigail Adams: Witness to a Revolution* by Natalie S. Bober.
        Illustration: *John Henry* retold by Julius Lester, ill. by Jerry Pinkney.

1994   Fiction: *Scooter* by Vera Williams.
        Nonfiction: *Eleanor Roosevelt* by Russell Freedman.
        Illustration: *Grandfather's Journey* by Allen Say.

1993   Fiction: *Ajeemah and His Son* by James Berry.
        Honor Book: *The Giver* by Lois Lowry.
        Nonfiction: *Sojourner Truth: Ain't I a Woman?* by Patricia C. McKissack and Fredrick McKissack.
        Illustration: *Fortune Teller* by Lloyd Alexander.

1992   Fiction: *Missing May* by Cynthia Rylant.
        Nonfiction: *Talking with Artists* by Pat Cummings.
        Illustration: *Seven Blind Mice* by Ed Young.

1991   Fiction: *The True Confessions of Charlotte Doyle* by Avi.
        Nonfiction: *Appalachia: The Voices of Sleeping Birds* by Cynthia Rylant.
        Illustration: *The Tale of the Mandarin Duck* by Katherine Paterson, ill. by Leo Dillon and Diane Dillon.

1990   Fiction: *Maniac Magee* by Jerry Spinelli.
        Nonfiction: *The Great Little Madison* by Jean Fritz.
        Illustration: *Lon Po Po* by Ed Young.

1989   Fiction: *The Village By The Sea* by Paula Fox.
        Nonfiction: *The Way Things Work* by David Macaulay.
        Illustration: *Shy Charles* by Rosemary Wells.

GOLDEN KITE AWARDS

Established in 1973 by the Society of Children's Book Writers, it is presented annually to those who "best exhibit excellence in writing or illustration and genuinely appeal to the interests and concerns of children."

1994   Fiction: *Catherine Called Birdy* by Karen Cushman.
        Nonfiction: *Kids at Work: Lewis Hine and the Crusade Against Child Labor* by Russell Freedman.

1993 Fiction: *Make Lemonade* by Virginia Euwer Wolff.
Nonfiction: *Eleanor Roosevelt: A Life of Discovery* by Russell Freedman.
Picture-Illustration: *By the Light of the Halloween Moon* by Kevin Hawkes.

1992 Fiction: *Letters from a Slave Girl: The Harriet Jacobs Story* by Mary E. Lyons.
Nonfiction: *The Long Road to Gettysburg* by Jim Murphy.
Picture-Illustration: *Chicken Sunday* by Patricia Polacco.

1991 Fiction: *The Raincatchers* by Jean Thesman.
Nonfiction: *The Wright Brothers: How They Invented the Airplane* by Russell Freedman.
Picture-Illustration: *Mama, Do You Love Me?* by Barbara M. Joosse, ill. by Barbara Lavellee.

1990 Fiction: *The True Confessions of Charlotte Doyle* by Avi.
Nonfiction: *The Boy's War: Confederate and Union Soldiers Talk About the Civil War* by Jim Murphy.
Picture-Illustration: *Home Place by Crescent Dragonwagon*, ill. by Jerry Pinkney.

1989 Fiction: *Jenny of the Tetons* by Kristiana Gregory.
Nonfiction: *Panama Canal: Gateway to the World* by Judith St. George.
Picture-Illustration: *Tom Thumb* by Richard Jesse Watson.

IRA CHILDREN'S BOOK AWARD WINNERS

Since 1987 the International Reading Association has recognized a book in a young adult or older reader category.

1995 *Spite Fence* by Trudy Krisher.

1994 *Behind the Secret Window, A Memoir of a Secret Childhood During World War Two* by Nelly S. Toll.

1993 *Letters from Rifka* by Karen Hesse.

1992 *Rescue Josh McGuire* by Ben Mikaelsen.

1991 *Under the Hawthorn Tree* by Marita Conlon-Mckenna.

1990 *Children of the River* by Linda Crew.

1989 *Probably Still Nick Swansen* by Virginia Euwer Wolff.

CORETTA SCOTT KING AWARD

Begun in 1969, this award is designed to "commemorate and foster the life, works and dreams" of Dr. Martin Luther King Jr., and to honor Mrs. King for "her courage and determination to continue the work for peace and world brotherhood."

1996 *Her Stories* by Virginia Hamilton. Illustrated by Leo Dillon and Diane Dillon.
Honor Books
The Watsons Go to Birmingham—1963 by Christopher Paul Curtis.
Like Sisters on the Homefront by Rita Williams-Garcia.
From the Notebooks of the Meianin Sun by Jacqueline Woodson.

1995 *Christmas in the Big House, Christmas in the Quarters* by Patricia C. McKissack and Fredrick L. McKissack.
Honor Books
I Hadn't Meant to Tell You This by Jacqueline Woodson.
Black Diamond: The Story of the Negro Baseball League by Patricia C. McKissack and Fredrick L. McKissack, Jr.
The Captive by Joyce Hansen.

1994 *Toning the Sweep* by Angela Johnson.
Soul Looks Back in Wonder by Tom Feelings.
Honor Books
Malcolm X: By Any Means Necessary by Walter Dean Myers.
Brown Honey in Broomwheat Tea by Joyce Carol Thomas.

1993 *The Dark-Thirty: Southern Tales of the Supernatural* by Patricia McKissack.
Honor Books
Somewhere in the Darkness by Walter Dean Myers.
Mississippi Challenge by Mildred Pitts Walter.
Sojourner Truth: Ain't I a Woman? by Patricia McKissack and Fredrick McKissack.

1992 *Now Is Your Time: The African American Struggle for Freedom* by Walter Dean Myers.
Tar Beach by Faith Ringold.
Honor Books
Night on Neighborhood Street by Eloise Greenfield.
All Day, All Night: A Child's First Book of African American Spirituals selected by Ashley Bryan.

1991 *The Road to Memphis* by Mildred Taylor.
Aida told by Leontine Price, ill. by Leo Dillon and Diane Dillon.
Honor Books
Black Dance in America: A History Through Its People by Jim Haskins.
When I Am Old with You by Angela Johnson.

1990 *A Long Hard Journey: The Story of the Pullman Porter* by Patricia McKissack and Fredrick McKissack.
Nathaniel Talking by Eloise Greenfield, ill. by Jan Spivey Gilchrist.
Honor Books
The Bells of Christmas by Virginia Hamilton.
Martin Luther King, Jr., and the Freedom Movement by Lillie Patterson.
The Talking Eggs by Robert D. San Souci.

1989 *Fallen Angels* by Walter D. Myers.
Mirandy and Brother Wind by Patricia McKissack, ill. by Jerry Pinkney.
Honor Books
A Thief in the Village and Other Stories by James Berry.
Anthony Burns: The Defeat and Triumph of a Fugitive Slave by Virginia Hamilton.

NATIONAL JEWISH BOOK AWARDS

Begun in 1952 by the Jewish Book Council to "encourage and award the author of an original, English publication for children, which embraces a Jewish theme, or to recognize the cumulative work of an author's contribution to Jewish juvenile literature."

1995 *Under the Domim Tree* by Gila Almago.

1993 No award was given.

1992 *The Man from the Other Side* by Uri Orlev, translated by Hillel Halkin.
Chicken Man by Michelle Edwards.

1991 *Becoming Gershona* by Nava Semel.
Hanukkah by Roni Schotter, ill. by Marylin Hafner.

1990 *Number the Stars* by Lois Lowry.
Berchick by Esther Silverstein Blanc, ill. by Tennessee Dixon.

1989 *Devil's Arithmetic* by Jane Yolen.
Just Enough Is Plenty: A Hanukkah Tale by Barbara Diamond Goldin, ill. by Seymour Chwast.

NEWBERY MEDAL BOOKS

The Newbery Award was established in 1922 in honor of the English publisher and bookseller, John Newbery. It is presented annually by the American Library Association to "the author of the most distinguished contribution to American literature for children" published in the preceding year. The winning book is awarded the Newbery Medal and one or more runners-up are designed as Honor Books.

1996 *The Midwife's Apprentice* by Karen Cushman.
Honor Books
What Jamie Saw by Carolyn Coman.
The Watsons Go to Birmingham—1963 by Christopher Paul Curtis.
Yolanda's Genius by Carol Fenner.
The Great Fire by Jim Murphy.

1995 *Walk Two Moons* by Sharon Creech.
Honor Books
Catherine Called Birdy by Karen Cushman.
The Ear, the Eye and the Arm by Nancy Farmer.

1994 *The Giver* by Lois Lowry.
Honor Books
Crazy Lady by Jane Leslie Conly.
Dragon's Gate by Laurence Yep.
Eleanor Roosevelt: A Life of Discovery by Russell Freedman.

1993 *Missing May* by Cynthia Rylant.
Honor Books
The Dark-Thirty: Southern Tales of the Supernatural by Patricia McKissack.
Somewhere in the Darkness by Walter Dean Myers.
What Hearts by Bruce Brooks.

1992 *Shiloh* by Phyllis Reynolds Naylor.
Honor Books
Nothing but the Truth by Avi.
The Wright Brothers: How They Invented the Airplane by Russell Freedman.

1991 *Maniac Magee* by Jerry Spinelli.
Honor Book
The True Confessions of Charlotte Doyle by Avi.

1990 *Number the Stars* by Lois Lowry.
Honor Books
Afternoon of the Elves by Janet Taylor Lisel.
Shabanu, Daughter of the Wind by Susan Fisher Staples.
The Winter Room. by Gary Paulsen.

1989 *Joyful Noise: Poems for Two Voices* by Paul Fleischman.
Honor Books
In the Beginning: Creation Stories from Around the World by Virginia Hamilton.
Scorpions by Walter Dean Myers.

SCOTT O'DELL AWARD FOR HISTORICAL FICTION

This award was originated and donated by Scott O'Dell in 1981 for a distinguished work of historical fiction. "The book content must be historical fiction set in the new world and have literary merit."

1995 *Under the Blood Red Sun* by Graham Salisbury.

1994 *Bull Run* by Paul Fleischman.

1993 *Morning Girl* by Michael Dorris.

1992 *Stepping on the Cracks* by Mary Dowling Hahn.

1991 *Time of Troubles* by Pieter Van Raven.

1990 *Shades of Gray* by Carolyn Reeder.

1989 *Honorable Prison* by Lylle DeJenkins.

ORBIS PICTUS

Given annually since 1990 by the National Council of Teachers of English, the award honors distinction in nonfiction for children. It commemorates *Orbis Pictus* by Johannes Amos Commenius, which is considered to be the first work of nonfiction exclusively for young readers.

1995 *Safari: Beneath the Sea: The Wonder World of North Pacific Coast* by Diane Swanson.
Honor Books
Wildlife Rescue: The Work of Dr. Kathleen Ramsey by Jennifer Owings Dewey.
Kids at Work: Lew Hine and the Crusade Against Child Labor by Russell Freeman.
Christmas in the Big House, Christmas in the Quarters by Patricia C. McKissack and Fredrick L. McKissack.

1994 *Crossing America on an Immigrant Train* by Jim Murphy.
Honor Books
To the Top of the World: Adventures with Arctic Wolves by Jim Brandenburg.
Making Sense: Animal Perception and Communication by Bruce Brooks.

1993 *Children of the Dust Bowl: The True Story of the School at Weed Patch Camp* by Jerry Stanley.
Honor Books
Talking with Artists by Pat Cummings.
Come Back Salmon by Molly Cone.

1992 *Flight: The Journey of Charles Lindbergh* by Robert Burleigh, ill. by Mike Wimmer.
Honor Books
Now Is Your Time: The African American Struggle for Freedom by Walter Dean Myers.
Prairie Vision: The Life and Times of Solomon Butcher by Pam Conrad.

1991 *Franklin Delano Roosevelt* by Russell Freedman.
Honor Books
Arctic Memories by Normee Ekoomiak.
Seeing the Earth from Space by Patricia Lauber.

1990 *The Great Little Madison* by Jean Fritz.
Honor Books
The Great American Gold Rush by Rhoda Blumberg.
The News About Dinosaurs by Patricia Lauber.

CARTER G. WOODSON BOOK AWARD

This award was established in 1973 by the National Council for the Social Studies in honor of Harvard University Professor of History Carter G. Woodson known as the "father of American black history." The award recognizes trade books that provide a "multicultural or multiethnic perspective." From 1989 to the present two awards have been given on both an elementary and secondary level. These are indicated with an E or S following the author's name.

1995 *What I Had Was Singing: The Story of Marian Anderson* by Jeri Ferria (E).
Till Victory Is Won: Black Soldiers in the Civil War by Zak Mettger (S).

1994 *Starting Home: The Story of Horace Pippin, Painter* by Mary E. Lyons (E).
The March on Washington by James Haskins (S).

1993 *Madame C. J. Walker* by Patricia and Fredrick McKissack (E).
Mississippi Challenge by Mildred Pitts Walter (S).

1992 *The Last Princess: The Story of Ka'iulani of Hawaii* by Fay Stanley (E).
Native American Doctor: The Story of Susan LaFlesche Picotte by Jeri Ferris (S).

1991 *Shirley Chisholm: Teacher and Congresswoman* by Catherine Scheader (E).
Sorrow's Kitchen: Zora Hurston by Mary Lyon (S).

1990 *In Two Worlds: A Yup'ik Eskimo Family* by Aylette Jenness and Alice Rivers (E).
Paul Robeson: Hero Before His Time by Rebecca Larsen (S).

1989 *Walking the Road to Freedom: A Story About Sojourner Truth* by Jeri Ferris (E).
Marian Anderson by Charles Patterson (S).

Professional References

Au, K. H. *Literacy Instruction in Multicultural Settings.* Orlando, FL: Harcourt Brace Jovanovich, 1993.

Banks, J. A. *An Introduction to Multicultural Education.* Boston: Allyn and Bacon, 1994.

Brown, J. E., and E. C. Stephens. *Teaching Young Adult Literature: Sharing the Connections.* Belmont, CA: Wadsworth, 1995.

Crawford, L. W. *Language and Literacy Learning in Multicultural Classrooms.* Boston: Allyn and Bacon, 1993.

Day, Frances Ann. *Multicultural Voices in Contemporary Literature: A Resource for Teachers.* Portsmouth, NH: Heinemann, 1994.

Harris, V. J., editor. *Teaching Multicultural Literature in Grades K-8.* Norwood, MA: Christopher-Gordon, 1993.

Johnson, L., and S. Smith. *Dealing with Diversity Through Multicultural Fiction: Library-Classroom.* Chicago: American Library Association, 1993.

Kirk, E. *The Black Experience in Books for Children and Young Adults.* Ardmore, OK: Positive Impact, 1993.

Miller, S. M., and B. McCaskill, eds. *Multicultural Literature and Literacies: Making Space for Difference.* Albany: State University of New York Press, 1993.

Palmer, B. C., M. L. Hafner, and M. F. Sharp. *Developing Cultural Literacy Through the Writing Process: Empowering All Learners.* Boston: Allyn and Bacon, 1994.

Rochman, Hazel. *Against Borders: Promoting Books for a Multicultural World.* Chicago: American Library Association, 1993.

References

Across Cultures

Bode, Janet. *New Kids in Town, Oral Histories of Immigrant Teens.* New York: Scholastic, 1989. 126 pages.

Fox, Paula. *The Slave Dancer.* New York: Dell, 1973. 127 pages.

Johnston, Johanna. *They Led the Way, 14 American Women.* New York: Scholastic, 1973. 126 pages.

Keehn, Sally M. *I Am Regina.* New York: Dell Yearling, 1991. 240 pages.

Levine, Ellen. . . . *If Your Name Was Changed at Ellis Island*. New York: Scholastic, 1993. 80 pages.

Lord, Bette Bao. *In the Year of the Boar and Jackie Robinson*. New York: Harper & Row, 1984. 169 pages.

Murphy, Jim. *Crossing America on an Immigrant Train*. New York: Clarion Books, 1993. 150 pages.

Perl, Lila. *The Great Ancestor Hunt: The Fun of Finding Out Who You Are*. New York: Clarion Books, 1989. 104 pages.

Sandler, Martin W. *Pioneers, A Library of Congress Book*. New York: HarperCollins, 1994.

Spinelli, Jerry. *Maniac Magee*. New York: HarperCollins, 1990. 184 pages.

Stein, R. Conrad. *The Bill of Rights*. Chicago: Children's Press, 1992.

Wolff, Virginia Euwer. *Make Lemonade*. New York: Henry Holt & Co., 1993. 200 pages.

African American

Boyd, Candy Dawson. *Circle of Gold*. New York: Scholastic, 1984. 124 pages.

Collier, James Lincoln, and Christopher Collier. *Jump Ship to Freedom*. New York: Dell, 1981. 198 pages.

———. *War Comes to Willy Freeman*. New York: Dell Yearling, 1983. 178 pages.

———. *Who Is Carrie?* New York: Dell Yearling, 1984. 158 pages.

Cornell, Jean Gay. *Louis Armstrong, Ambassador Satchmo*. New York: Dell Yearling, 1972. 96 pages.

Davis, Ossie. *Just Like Martin*. New York: Puffin Books, 1995. 215 pages.

Ferris, Jeri. *Walking the Road to Freedom: A Story About Sojourner Truth*. Minneapolis, MN: CarolRhoda Books, 1988. 64 pages.

Freedman, Florence. *Two Tickets to Freedom: The True Story of William and Ellen Craft, Fugitive Slaves*. New York: Scholastic, 1971. 96 pages.

Greenfield, Eloise. *Koya DeLaney and the Good Girl Blues*. New York: Scholastic, 1992. 124 pages.

Guy, Rosa. *The Friends*. New York: Bantam, 1973. 185 pages.

Hamilton, Virginia. *Anthony Burns: The Defeat and Triumph of a Fugitive Slave*. New York: Alfred A. Knopf, 1988. 193 pages.

———. *Cousins*. New York: Philomel Books, 1990. 125 pages.

———. *The House of Dies Drear*. New York: Collier Books, 1968. 279 pages.

———. *Paul Robeson, The Life and Times of a Free Black Man*. New York: Dell, 1974. 224 pages.

———. *Plain City*. New York: Scholastic, 1993. 193 pages.

Hansen, Joyce. *Between 2 Fires: Black Soldiers in the Civil War*. New York: Franklin Watts, 1993. 160 pages.

———. *The Captive*. New York: Scholastic, 1994. 195 pages.

———. *The Gift-Giver*. New York: Clarion Books, 1980. 188 pages.

———. *Home Boy*. New York: Clarion Books, 1982. 181 pages.

———. *Yellow Bird and Me*. New York: Clarion Books, 1986. 155 pages.

———. *Out from This Place*. New York: Avon, 1988. 135 pages.

———. *Which Way Freedom?* New York: Avon, 1986. 120 pages.

Haskins, Jim. *One More River to Cross, The Stories of Twelve Black Americans*. New York: Scholastic, 1992. 215 pages.

———. *Outward Dream, Black Inventors and Their Inventions*. New York: Bantam, 1991. 101 pages.

Krug, Elisabeth. *Thurgood Marshall, Champion of Civil Rights*. New York: Ballantine Books, 1993. 147 pages.

Lester, Julius. *Long Journey Home*. New York: Scholastic, 1972. 150 pages.

Levine, Ellen. *Freedom's Children, Young Civil Rights Activists Tell Their Own Stories*. New York: Avon Books, 1993. 204 pages.

Lyons, Mary E. *Letters from a Slave Girl, The Story of Harriet Jacobs*. New York: Charles Scribner's Sons, 1992. 146 pages.

McCurdy, Michael, editor and illustrator. *Escape from Slavery, The Boyhood of Frederick Douglass in His Own Words*. New York: Alfred A. Knopf, 1994. 63 pages.

McKissack, Patricia C., and Fredrick McKissack. *Madame C. J. Walker: Self-Made Millionaire*. Hillside, NJ: Enslow, 1992.

———. *Sojourner Truth, Ain't I a Woman?* New York: Scholastic, 1992. 186 pages.

McKissack, Patricia C., and Fredrick McKissack, Jr. *Black Diamond, The Story of the Negro Baseball Leagues*. New York: Scholastic, 1994. 184 pages.

Meltzer, Milton. *Mary McLeod Bethune, Voice of Black Hope*. New York: Puffin Books, 1987. 57 pages.

Meyer, Carolyn. *White Lilacs*. San Diego: Harcourt Brace & Co., 1993. 242 pages.

Moore, Eva. *The Story of George Washington Carver*. New York: Scholastic, 1971. 96 pages.

Moore, Yvette. *Freedom Songs*. New York: Puffin Books, 1991. 168 pages.

Myers, Walter Dean. *Fast Sam, Cool Clyde, and Stuff*. New York: Puffin, 1975. 190 pages.

——. *The Glory Field*. New York: Scholastic Books, 1994.

——. *Hoops*. New York: Dell, 1981. 183 pages.

——. *Malcolm X, By Any Means Necessary*. New York: Scholastic, 1993. 210 pages.

——. *Motown and Didi*. New York: Dell, 1984. 174 pages.

——. *Now Is Your Time! The African-American Struggle for Freedom*. New York: Scholastic, 1991. 292 pages.

——. *The Outside Shot*. New York: Dell, 1984. 185 pages.

——. *Scorpions*. New York: Harper & Row, 1988. 216 pages.

——. *Somewhere in the Darkness*. New York: Scholastic, 1992. 168 pages.

——. *Won't Know Till I Get There*. New York: Puffin Books, 1982. 176 pages.

Paulsen, Gary. *NIGHTJOHN*. New York: Delacorte Press, 1993. 92 pages.

Petry, Ann. *Tituba of Salem Village*. New York: HarperCollins, 1964, 1992. 254 pages.

Rappaport, Doreen. *Escape from Slavery, Five Journeys to Freedom*. New York: HarperCollins, 1991. 117 pages.

Rupert, Janet. *The African Mask*. New York: Clarion Books, 1994. 125 pages.

Scheader, Catherine. *Shirley Chisholm: Teacher and Congresswoman*. Springfield, NJ: Enslow Pub., 1990. 128 pages.

Sebestyen, Ouida. *Words By Heart*. New York: Bantam Books, 1968, 1979. 135 pages.

Siegel, Beatrice. *The Year They Walked*. New York: Four Winds Press, 1991. 103 pages.

Smothers, Ethel Footman. *Down in the Piney Woods*. New York: Random House, 1992. 151 pages.

Stein, R. Conrad. *The Montgomery Bus Boycott*. Chicago: Children's Press, 1993.

Sterling, Dorothy. *Freedom Train, The Story of Harriet Tubman*. New York: Scholastic, 1954. 191 pages.

Tate, Eleanora E. *A Blessing in Disguise*. New York: Delacorte Press, 1995. 184 pages.

——. Illustrated by Eric Velasquez. *Front Porch Stories at the One-Room School*. New York: Bantam Books, 1992. 98 pages.

——. *The Secret of Gumbo Grove*. New York: Bantam Books, 1987. 199 pages.

——. *Thank You, Dr. Martin Luther King, Jr.!* New York: Bantam Books, 1990. 237 pages.

Taylor, Mildred D. *Song of the Trees.* New York: Bantam Books, 1975. 52 pages.

——. *The Friendship.* New York: Bantam Skylark, 1987. 47 pages.

Turner, Glennette Tilley. *Take a Walk in Their Shoes.* New York: Puffin Books, 1989. 174 pages.

Walker, Mildren Pitts. *Mississippi Challenge.* New York: Bradbury Press, 1992. 205 pages.

Williams-Garcia, Rita. *Blue Tights.* New York: Bantam Books, 1988. 138 pages.

——. *Fast Talk on a Slow Train.* New York: Bantam Books, 1991. 182 pages.

Wilson, Johnniece Marshall. *Oh, Brother.* New York: Scholastic, 1988. 121 pages.

Yates, Elizabeth. *Amos Fortune, Free Man.* New York: Puffin Books, 1950. 181 pages.

Asian

Choi, Sook Nyul. *Year of Impossible Goodbyes.* New York: Dell Yearling, 1991. 169 pages.

——. *Echoes of the White Giraffe.* Boston: Houghton Mifflin, 1993. 137 pages.

Coerr, Eleanor. *Sadako and the Thousand Paper Cranes.* New York: Dell, 1977. 64 pages.

Garland, Sherry. *Song of the Buffalo Boy.* San Diego: Harcourt Brace & Co., 1994. 282 pages.

Ho, Minfong. *The Clay Marble.* New York: Farrar, Straus & Giroux, 1991. 150 pages.

Mori, Kyoko. *Shizuko's Daughter.* New York: Henry Holt & Co., 1993. 227 pages.

Nhuong, Huynh Quang. *The Land I Lost, Adventures of a Boy in Vietnam.* New York: HarperCollins, 1982. 127 pages.

Whelan, Gloria. *Goodbye, Vietnam.* New York: Alfred A. Knopf, 1992. 136 pages.

Asian American

Crew, Linda. *Children of the River.* New York: Dell Publishing, 1989. 213 pages.

Garland, Sherry. *Shadow of the Dragon.* San Diego: Harcourt Brace & Co., 1993. 314 pages.

Houston, Jeanne Wakatsuki, and James D. Houston. *Farewell to Manzanar.* New York: Bantam Books, 1973. 145 pages.

Howard, Ellen. *Her Own Song.* New York: Macmillan, 1988. 160 pages.

Hoyt-Goldsmith, Diane. Photographs by Lawrence Migdale. *Hoang Anh, A Vietnamese-American Boy.* New York: Scholastic, 1992. 32 pages.

Lee, Marie. *Finding My Voice*. Boston: Houghton Mifflin, 1992. 163 pages.

Namioka, Lensey. *April and the Dragon Lady*. San Diego: Harcourt Brace & Co., 1994. 214 pages.

———. *Yang the Youngest and His Terrible Ear*. New York: Dell, 1992. 134 pages.

Okimoto, Jean Davies. *Molly by Any Other Name*. New York: Scholastic, 1990. 276 pages.

Petti, Jayne. *My Name Is San Ho*. New York: Scholastic, 1992. 149 pages.

Uchida, Yoshiko. *Journey Home*. New York: Aladdin Books, 1978. 131 pages.

———. *A Jar of Dreams*. New York: Macmillan, 1981. 144 pages.

Yep, Laurence. *Child of the Owl*. New York: HarperCollins, 1977. 217 pages.

———. *Dragon's Gate*. New York: HarperCollins, 1993. 273 pages.

———. *Dragonwings*. New York: Harper & Row, 1975. 248 pages.

Caribbean Islands

Berry, James. *Ajeemah and His Son*. New York: HarperCollins, 1991. 83 pages.

Dorris, Michael. *Morning Girl*. New York: Hyperion Books, 1991. 74 pages.

O'Dell, Scott. *My Name Is Not Angelica*. New York: Dell Yearling, 1989. 130 pages.

Taylor, Theodore. *The Cay*. New York: Avon Books, 1969. 144 pages.

———. *Timothy of the Cay, A Prequel-Sequel*. San Diego: Harcourt Brace & Co., 1993. 161 pages.

Central America

Buss, Fran Leeper with the assistance of Daisy Cubias. *Journey of the Sparrows*. New York: Dell Yearling, 1991. 155 pages.

Castanda, Omar S. *Among the Volcanoes*. New York: Dell Yearling, 1991. 183 pages.

Moeri, Louise. *The Forty-Third War*. Boston: Houghton Mifflin Co., 1989. 200 pages.

Eastern European

Filipovic, Zlata. Translated by Christina Pribichevich-Zoric. *Zlata's Diary, A Child's Life in Sarajevo*. New York: Viking, 1994. 200 pages.

European American

Bauer, Marion Dane. *A Dream of Queens and Castles*. New York: Clarion Books, 1990. 118 pages.

———. *A Question of Trust*. New York: Scholastic, 1994. 130 pages.

———. *A Taste of Smoke*. New York: Clarion Books, 1993. 106 pages.

———. *Face to Face*. New York: Clarion Books, 1991. 176 pages.

———. *On My Honor*. New York: Dell Publishing, 1986. 90 pages.

Blos, Joan W. *A Gathering of Days*. New York: Aladdin Books, 1979. 144 pages.

Bridgers, Sue Ellen. *Keeping Christina*. New York: HarperCollins, 1993. 281 pages.

———. *Permanent Connections*. New York: Harper & Row, 1987. 264 pages.

Carter, Alden R. *Up Country*. New York: Scholastic, 1989. 256 pages.

Cole, Brock. *Celine*. New York: Farrar, Straus & Giroux, 1989. 216 pages.

———. *The Goats*. New York: Farrar, Straus & Giroux, 1987. 184 pages.

Conly, Jane Leslie. *Crazy Lady*. New York: HarperCollins, 1993. 180 pages.

Crutcher, Chris. *The Crazy Horse Electric Game*. New York: Dell, 1987. 224 pages.

———. *Staying Fat for Sarah Byrnes*. New York: Greenwillow Books, 1993. 216 pages.

———. *Stotan!* New York: Dell Publishing, 1986. 183 pages.

Duffy, James. *Radical Red*. New York: Charles Scribner's Sons, 1993. 152 pages.

Fenner, Carol. *Randall's Wall*. New York: Bantam Skylark, 1991. 85 pages.

Hahn, Mary Downing. *Stepping on the Cracks*. New York: Clarion Books, 1991. 216 pages.

Hobbs, Will. *Downriver*. New York: Bantam Books, 1991. 204 pages.

MacLachlan, Patricia. *Journey*. New York: Dell, 1991. 83 pages.

Mazer, Harry. *When the Phone Rang*. New York: Scholastic, 1985. 181 pages.

Mazer, Norma Fox. *After the Rain*. New York: Avon Books, 1987. 249 pages.

Naylor, Phyllis Reynolds. *Reluctantly Alice*. New York: Dell Publishing, 1991. 182 pages.

———. *Send No Blessing*. New York: Puffin Books, 1990.

Moscinski, Sharon. *Tracing Our Irish Roots*. Santa Fe, NM: John Muir Publications, 1993.

Peck, Richard. *Princess Ashley*. New York: Dell Publishing, 1987. 208 pages.

————. *Remembering the Good Times*. New York: Dell Publishing, 1985. 181 pages.

Rylant, Cynthia. *Missing May*. New York: Orchard Books, 1992. 89 pages.

Voight, Cynthia. *Dicey's Song*. New York: Ballantine Books, 1982. 211 pages.

Wolff, Virginia Euwer. *Probably Still Nick Swansen*. New York: Henry Holt & Co., 1988. 144 pages.

European Immigrant

Angell, Judie. *One Way to Ansonia*. New York: Berkley Books, 1985. 183 pages.

Colman, Hila. *Rachel's Legacy*. New York: William Morrow & Co., 1978. 190 pages.

Gross, Virginia T. *It's Only Goodbye, An Immigrant Story*. New York: Puffin Books, 1990. 54 pages.

Freedman, Russell. *Immigrant Children*. New York: Scholastic, 1980. 72 pages.

Koller, Jackie French. *Nothing to Fear*. San Diego: Harcourt Brace Jovanovich, 1991. 279 pages.

Nixon, Joan Lowery. *A Family Apart*. New York: Bantam Books, 1987. 162 pages.

————. *A Place to Belong*. New York: Bantam Books, 1989. 147 pages.

————. *Land of Dreams*. New York: Delacorte Press, 1994. 153 pages.

————. *Land of Hope*. New York: Dell, 1992. 171 pages.

————. *Land of Promise*. New York: Dell, 1992. 169 pages.

Stein, R. Conrad. *Ellis Island*. Chicago: Children's Press, 1992.

Hawaiian American

Salisbury, Graham. *Blue Skin of the Sea*. New York: Delacorte Press, 1992. 215 pages.

————. *Under the Blood-Red Sun*. New York: Delacorte Press, 1994. 246 pages.

Holocaust

Adler, David A. *We Remember the Holocaust*. New York: Henry Holt & Co., 1989. 148 pages.

Isaacman, Clara, as told to Joan Adess Grossman. *Clara's Story*. New York: The Jewish Publication Society of America, 1984. 120 pages.

Lowry, Lois. *Number the Stars*. New York: Dell Yearling, 1989. 137 pages.

Matas, Carol. *Daniel's Story*. New York: Scholastic, published in conjunction with the United States Holocaust Memorial Museum, 1993. 136 pages.

Orgel, Doris. *The Devil in Vienna*. New York: Dial Press, 1978. 246 pages.

Orlev, Uri. Translated from the Hebrew by Hillel Halkin. *The Man from the Other Side*. Boston: Houghton Mifflin Co., 1989, 1991. 186 pages.

Reiss, Johanna. *The Upstairs Room*. New York: Thomas Y. Crowell, 1972. 179 pages.

Richter, Hans Peter, translated from the German by Edite Kroll. *Friedrich*. New York: Puffin Books, 1961, 1970. 140 pages.

Sachs, Marilyn. *A Pocket Full of Seeds*. New York: Puffin Books, 1973. 137 pages.

Siegal, Aranka. *Upon the Head of a Goat*. New York: Puffin Books, 1981. 215 pages.

Yolen, Jane. *Devil's Arithmetic*. New York: Puffin Books, 1988. 170 pages.

Inuit

George, Jean Craighead. *Julie of the Wolves*. New York: HarperCollins, 1972. 170 pages.

———. *Water Sky*. New York: HarperCollins, 1987. 212 pages.

Rogers, Jean. *Goodbye, My Island*. New York: Greenwillow Books, 1993. 83 pages.

Jewish

Boraks-Nemetz, Lillian. *The Old Brown Suitcase: A Teenager's Story of War and Peace*. Port Angeles, WA: Ben-Simon Publications, 1994. 148 pages.

Lasky, Kathy. *The Night Journey*. New York: Puffin Books, 1981. 150 pages.

Levitin, Sonia. *Journey to America*. New York: Scholastic, 1970. 150 pages.

Levoy, Myron. *Alan and Naomi*. New York: Dell, 1977. 176 pages.

Sagan, Miriam. *Tracing Our Jewish Roots*. Santa Fe, NM: John Muir Publications, 1993.

Semel, Nava. Translated by Semour Simckes. *Becoming Gershona*. New York: Puffin Books, 1990. 153 pages.

Mexico

Beatty, Patricia. *Lupita Manana*. New York: Beech Tree Books, Wm. Morrow, 1981. 190 pages.

Behrens, June. *Fiesta: Cinco de Mayo*. Chicago: Children's Press, 1978.

Bruin, Mary Ann. *Rosita's Christmas Wish*. San Antonio, TX: TexArt Services, Inc., 1985.

Clendenen, Mary Jo. *Gonzalo: Coronado's Shepherd Boy*. Austin, TX: Eakin Press, 1990.

McColley, Kevin. *The Walls of Pedro Garcia*. New York: Delacorte Press, 1993. 100 pages.

Palacios, Argentia. *Viva Mexico! The Story of Benito Juarez and Cinco de Mayo*. Thompsonville, NY: Mariposa, 1993.

Mexican American

Anaya, Rudolfo. *Bless Me, Ultima*. Berkeley, CA: TQS Publications, 1872. 248 pages.

Bethancout, T. Ernesto. *The Me Inside of Me*. Minneapolis, MN: Lerner Publications, 1985.

Buss, Fran Leeper with the assistance of Daisy Cubias. *Journey of the Sparrows*. New York: Dell Yearling, 1991. 155 pages.

Krumgold, Joseph. *. . . And Now Miguel*. New York: Scholastic, 1953. 245 pages.

Meltzer, M. *The Hispanic Americans*. New York: Thomas Y. Crowell, 1982. 149 pages.

Roberts, Maurice. *Henry Cisneros: A Leader for the Future*. Chicago: Children's Press, 1991.

Soto, Gary. *Living up the Street*. New York: Dell, 1985. 167 pages.

———. *Local News*. San Diego: Harcourt Brace Jovanovich, 1993. 148 pages.

———. *Small Faces*. New York: Dell, 1986. 137 pages.

———. *Taking Sides*. San Diego: Harcourt Brace Jovanovich, 1991. 138 pages.

Vigil, Angel. Translated by Jennifer Audrey Lowell and Juan Francisco Marín. *The Corn Woman: Stories and Legends of the Hispanic Southwest*. Englewood, CO: Libraries Unlimited, Inc., 1994. 234 pages.

Middle East

Staples, Suzanne Fisher. *Haveli*. New York: Alfred A. Knopf, Inc., 1993. 259 pages.

———. *Shabanu, Daughter of the Wind*. New York: Alfred A. Knopf, 1989. 240 pages.

Native American

Bennett, James. *Dakota Dream*. New York: Scholastic, 1994. 182 pages.

Blos, Joan W. *Brothers of the Heart*. New York: Aladdin Books, 1985. 162 pages.

Carter, Alden. *Dogwolf*. New York: Scholastic, 1994. 231 pages.

Dowd, John. *Ring of Tall Trees*. Anchorage, AK: Alaska Northwest Books, 1992. 126 pages.

Hirschfelder, Arlene and Beverly R. Singer, selected by. *Rising Voices, Writings of Young Native Americans*. New York: Ivy Books, 1992. 131 pages.

Hobbs, Will. *Beardance*. New York: Atheneum, 1993. 197 pages.

——. *Bearstone*. New York: Atheneum, 1989. 154 pages.

Hudson, Jan. *Sweetgrass*. New York: Scholastic, 1984. 159 pages.

Krensky, Stephen. Illustrated by James Watling. *Children of the Wind and Water: Five Stories About Native American Children*. New York: Scholastic, 1994. 32 pages.

Major, Kevin. *Blood Red Ochre*. New York: Dell Publishing, 1989. 147 pages.

Munson, Sammye. *Our Tejano Heroes: Outstanding Mexican-Americans in Texas*. Austin, TX: Eakin Press, 1989.

Naylor, Phyllis Reynolds. *To Walk the Sky Path*. New York: Dell Yearling, 1973. 144 pages.

O'Dell, Scott. *Island of the Blue Dolphins*. New York: Dell, 1960. 189 pages.

——. *Sing Down the Moon*. New York: Dell, 1970. 124 pages.

O'Dell, Scott, and Elizabeth Hall. *Thunder Rolling in the Mountain*. New York: Dell Yearling, 1992. 128 pages.

Pitts, Paul. *Shadowman's Way*. New York: Avon Books, 1992. 120 pages.

Rand McNally Children's Atlas of Native American Cultures. Skokie, IL: Rand McNally, 1992. 77 pages.

Robinson, Margaret A. *A Woman of Her Tribe*. New York: A Fawcett Juniper Book, 1990. 148 pages.

Roop, Peter, and Connie Roop. Illustrated by Yoshi Mlyake. *Ahyoka and the Talking Leaves*. New York: Beech Tree, Wm. Morrow, 1994. 60 pages.

Speare, Elizabeth George. *The Sign of the Beaver*. New York: Dell, 1983. 135 pages.

Spinka, Penina Keen. *Mother's Blessing*. New York: Fawcett Juniper, 1992. 182 pages.

——. *White Hare's Horses*. New York: Fawcett Juniper, 1991. 161 pages.

Thomasma, Kenneth. *Naya Nuki, Shoshoni Girl Who Ran*. Grand Rapids, MI: Baker Book House Co., 1991. 175 pages.

Whelan, Gloria. *Night of the Full Moon*. New York: Alfred A. Knopf, 1993. 63 pages.

Russia

Bograd, Larry. *The Kolokol Papers*. New York: Dell, 1981. 168 pages.

Hautzig, Esther. *The Endless Steppe*. New York: HarperCollins, 1968. 243 pages.

Lasky, Kathryn. *The Night Journey*. New York: Puffin Books, 1981. 150 pages.

Matas, Carol. *Sworn Enemies*. New York: Dell, 1993. 132 pages.

South Africa

Gordon, Shelia. *The Middle of Somewhere, A Story of South Africa*. New York: Orchard Books, 1990. 154 pages.

———. *Waiting for the Rain*. New York: Bantam Books, 1987. 214 pages.

Turkey

Hiçyilmaz, Gaye. *Against the Storm*. New York: Dell Yearling, 1990. 200 pages.

Collections

Appleman, Deborah, and Margaret Appleman. *Braided Lives*. St. Paul: Minnesota Humanities Commission, 1991.

Bolden, Tonya, ed. *Rites of Passage, Stories About Growing up by Black Writers from Around the World*. New York: Hyperion Books for Children, 1994.

Carlson, Lori M., and Cynthia L. Ventura, eds. *Where Angels Glide at Dawn, New Stories from Latin America*. New York: HarperCollins, 1990.

Gallo, Donald R., ed. *Join In, Multiethnic Short Stories*. New York: Delacorte Press, 1993.

Mazer, Anne, ed. *America Street, A Multicultural Anthology of Stories*. New York: Persea Books, 1993.

Nye, Naomi Shihab, selected by. *This Same Sky, A Collection of Poems from Around the World*. New York: Four Winds Press, 1992.

Pettepiece, Thomas, and Anatoly Aleksin, ed. *Face to Face, A Collection of Stories by Celebrated Soviet and American Writers*. New York: Philomel Books, 1990.

Rochman, Hazel, selected by. *Somehow Tenderness Survives, Stories of Southern Africa*. New York: HarperCollins, 1988.

Soto, Gary. *A Fire in My Hands, A Book of Poems*. New York: Scholastic, 1990.

Strickland, Michael R., selected by. Illustrated by Alan Leiner. *Poems That Sing to You*. Honesdale, PA: Boyds Mill Press, 1993.

Thomas, Joyce Carol, ed. *A Gathering of Flowers, Stories About Being Young in America*. New York: HarperCollins, 1990.

Wilson, Budge. *The Leaving and Other Stories*. New York: Scholastic, 1990.

Folk Literature from Many Cultures

Aardema, Verna. *Borreguita and the Coyote: Tale from Ayutha, Mexico*. New York: Alfred A. Knopf, 1991.

Alexander, Lloyd. Illustrated by Trina Schart Hyman. *The Fortune-Tellers*. New York: Dutton Children's Press, 1992.

Bruchac, Joseph, and Jonathan London. Illustrated by Thomas Locker. *Thirteen Moons on Turtle's Back, A Native American Year of Moons*. New York: Philomel Books, 1992.

Climo, Shirley. Illustrated by Ruth Heller. *The Egyptian Cinderella*. New York: HarperCollins, 1989.

Coerr, Eleanor. Illustrated by Ed Young. *Sadako*. New York: G. P. Putnam's Sons, 1993.

Cohen, Caron Lee, retold by, illustrated by Shonto Begay. *The Mud Pony*. New York: Scholastic, 1988.

Cohlene, Terri, written and adapted by, illustrated by Charles Reasoner. *Little Firefly, An Algonquian Legend*. Mahwah, NY: Watermill Press, Troll Associates, 1990.

Cohlene, Terri. Illustrated by Charles Reasoner. *Quillworker, A Cheyenne Legend*. Mahwah, NY: Watermill Press, Troll Associates, 1990.

Esbensen, Barbara Juster, illustrated by Helen K. Davie. *The Star Maiden*. Boston: Little, Brown & Co., 1988.

Hamilton, Virginia. Illustrated by Jerry Pinkney. *Drylongso*. San Diego: Harcourt Brace Jovanovich, 1992.

———. *In the Beginning: Creation Stories from Around the World*. San Diego: Harcourt Brace Jovanovich, 1988.

———, told by. Illustrated by Leo Dillon and Diane Dillon. *The People Could Fly, American Black Folktales*. New York: Alfred A. Knopf, 1985.

Hayes, Joe. *The Day It Snowed Tortillas: Tales from Spanish New Mexico*. Thompsonville, NY: Mariposa, 1983.

———. *La Llorona: The Weeping Woman*. El Paso, TX: Cinco Puntos Press, 1987.

Joseph, Lynn. *The Mermaid's Twin Sister: More Stories from Trinidad*. New York: Clarion Books, 1994.

Lawson, Julie, retold by. Paintings by Paul Morin. *The Dragon's Pearl*. New York: Clarion Books, 1993.

Malotki, Ekkehart, retold by. Illustrated by Michael Lacapa. *The Mouse Couple, A Hopi Folktale*. Singapore: Northland Publishing, 1988.

McDermott, Gerald, adapted and illustrated by. *Arrow to the Sun, A Pueblo Indian Tale*. New York: Puffin Books, 1974.

McKissack, Patricia. *The Dark-Thirty, Southern Tales of the Supernatural*. New York: Alfred A. Knopf, 1992.

Rhoads, Dorothy. *The Corn Grows Ripe*. New York: Puffin Books, 1956, 1984.

Sis, Peter. *A Small Tall Tale from the Far Far North*. New York: Alfred A. Knopf, 1993.

Vuong, Lynette Dyer. *The Brocaded Slipper and Other Vietnamese Tales*. New York: Harper-Collins, 1992.

Yep, Laurence. *The Rainbow People*. New York: HarperCollins, 1989.

Young, Richard, and Judy Dockrey Young, collected and edited by. *African-American Folk-tales for Young Readers*. Little Rock, AR: August House, 1993.

Picture Books

Ancona, George. *Pablo Remembers, The Fiesta of the Day of the Dead*. New York: Lothrop, Lee & Shepard Books, 1993.

Brown, Tricia. Photographs by Kenneth Kobre. *L'Chaim: The Story of a Russian Emigre Boy*. New York: Henry Holt & Co., 1994.

Bruchac, Joseph. Illustrated by Paul Morin. *Fox Song*. New York: Philomel Books, 1993.

Bruchac, Joseph, and Jonathan London. Illustrated by Thomas Locker. *Thirteen Moons on Turtle's Back: A Native American Year of Moons*. New York: Philomel Books, 1992.

Bunting, Eve. Illustrated by Diane de Groat. *Sunshine Home*. New York: Clarion Books, 1994.

———. Illustrated by Ronald Himler. *A Day's Work*. New York: Clarion Books, 1994.

———. Illustrated by David Diaz. *Smoky Night*. San Diego: Harcourt Brace, 1994.

Collier, John. *The Backyard*. New York: Viking, 1993.

Flournoy, Valerie. Illustrated by Jerry Pinkney. *The Patchwork Quilt*. New York: Dial Books for Young Readers, 1985.

Fox, Mem. Illustrated by Julie Vivas. *Wilfrid Gordon McDonald Partridge*. New York: Kane/Miller Book Publishers, 1985.

Garland, Sherry. Illustrated by Tatsuro Kiuchi. *The Lotus Seed*. San Diego: Harcourt Brace Jovanovich, 1993.

Greenfield, Eloise. Illustrated by Jan Spivey Gilchrist. *First Pink Light*. New York: Writers and Readers Pub., 1976, 1991.

Feelings, Tom. *Soul Looks Back in Wonder*. New York: Dial Books, 1993.

Hausman, Gerald. Illustrated by Cara Moser and Barry Moser. *Turtle Island ABC, A Gathering of Native American Symbols*. New York: HarperCollins, 1994.

Heide, Florence Parry and Judith Heide Gilliland. Illustrated by Ted Lewin. *Sami and the Time of the Troubles*. New York: Clarion Books, 1992.

Johnson, Angela. Illustrated by David Soman. *When I am Old with You*. New York: Orchard Books, 1990.

Johnson, Dolores. *Now Let Me Fly, The Story of a Slave Family*. New York: Macmillan Publishing Co., 1993.

Kroll, Virginia. Illustrated by Katherine Roundtree. *Wood-Hoopoe Willie*. Watertown, MA: Charlesbridge Publishing, 1992.

Knight, Margy Burns. Illustrated by Anne Sibley O'Brien. *Who Belongs Here? An American Story*. Gardiner, ME: Tilbury House Publishers, 1993.

Lyon, George Ella. Illustrated by Peter Catalanotto. *Who Came Down That Road?* New York: Orchard Books, 1992.

MacLachlan, Patricia, pictures by Pertzoff. *Three Names*. New York: HarperCollins, 1991.

Mathis, Sharon Bell. Illustrated by Leo Dillon and Diane Dillon. *The Hundred Penny Box*. New York: Puffin Books, 1975.

McKissack, Patricia C., and Fredrick L. McKissack. Illustrated by John Thompson. *Christmas in the Big House, Christmas in the Quarters*. New York: Scholastic, 1994.

Miles, Miska. Illustrated by Peter Parnall. *Annie and the Old One*. Boston: Little, Brown, & Co., 1971.

Mochizuki, Ken. Illustrated by Dom Lee. *Baseball Saved Us*. New York: Lee & Low Books, 1993.

Mollel, Tololwa M. Illustrated by E. B. Lewis. *Big Boy*. New York: Clarion Books, 1995.

———. Illustrated by Barbara Spurll. *The Flying Tortoise: An Igbo Tale*. New York: Clarion Books, 1993.

Mora, Pat. Illustrated by Francisco X. Mora. *Listen to the Desert Oye al Desierto*. New York: Clarion Books, 1994.

Musgrove, Margaret. Pictures by Leo Dillon and Diane Dillon. *Ashanti to Zulu, African Traditions*. New York: Dial Books for Young Readers, 1976.

Myers, Walter Dean. *Brown Angels, An Album of Pictures and Verse*. New York: HarperCollins, 1993.

Nunes, Susan Miho. Illustrated by Chris K. Soentpiet. *The Last Dragon*. New York: Clarion Books, 1995.

Polacco, Patricia. *Chicken Sunday*. New York: Philomel Books, 1992.

———. *Mrs. Katz and Tush*. New York: Dell, 1992.

———. *The Keeping Quilt*. New York: Simon & Schuster, Inc., 1988.

Ringgold, Faith. *Aunt Harriet's Underground Railroad in the Sky*. New York: Crown Publishers, Inc., 1992.

Rylant, Cynthia. Illustrated by Barry Moser. *Appalachia, The Voices of Sleeping Birds*. San Diego: Harcourt Brace Jovanovich, 1991.

Say, Allen. *Grandfather's Journey*. Boston: Houghton Mifflin Co., 1993.

Stanek, Muriel. Illustrated by Judith Friedman. *I Speak English for My Mom*. Morton Grove, IL: Albert Whitman & Co., 1989.

Stanley, Fay. Illustrated by Diane Stanley. *The Last Princess: The Story of Ka'iulani of Hawai'i*. New York: Four Winds Press, 1991.

Williams, David. Illustrated by Wiktor Sadowski. *Grandma Essie's Covered Wagon*. New York: Alfred A. Knopf, 1993.

Winter, Jeanette. *Follow the Drinking Gourd*. New York: Alfred A. Knopf, 1988.

Wisniewski, David. *The Wave of the Sea-Wolf*. New York: Clarion, 1994.

Yolen, Jane. Illustrated by David Shannon. *Encounter*. San Diego: Harcourt Brace Jovanovich, 1992.

Index

About the Authors

Jean E. Brown

Jean E. Brown, Professor of Teacher Education at Saginaw Valley State University, is a former high school English teacher and department chair. She is a past president of the Michigan Council of Teachers of English and is former editor of the Council's newsletter, *The Michigan English Teacher*. From 1990 to 1993 she served on the SLATE Steering Committee of the National Council of Teachers of English and she currently chairs the Conference on English Education's Commission on Intellectual Freedom for NCTE. She has written over sixty articles and book chapters and has co-edited two teacher resource books with Elaine Stephens and Barbara Quirk, *Two Way Street: Integrating Reading and Writing in the Middle Schools* and *Two Way Street: Integrating Reading and Writing in the Secondary Schools*. She is also the co-author of *Toward Literacy: Theory and Practice in Teaching Writing in the Content Areas,* with Elaine C. Stephens and Lela Phillips (1993, Wadsworth Publishers). She and Dr. Stephens have completed their second textbook, *Young Adult Literature Sharing the Connections,* 1995, also from Wadsworth. She also is the contributing editor of a volume entitled *Preserving Intellectual Freedom: Fighting Censorship in Our Schools,* which was published in November 1994 by NCTE. She, Dr. Stephens, and Dr. Janet Rubin are also the co-authors of *Learning About the Holocaust . . . Literature and Other Resources* published by Library Professional Publications, Fall, 1995 and *Images from the Holocaust,* a literature anthology will be published in July 1996. She and Dr. Stephens are currently writing a classroom practices book for the National Council of Teachers of English entitled *United in Diversity: Multicultural Young Adult Literature*. She is the 1990 recipient of the C. C. Fries Award from Michigan Council of Teachers of English for service to the profession and the Saginaw Valley State University Faculty Association Award for Scholarly Achievement. In 1992 she received the Research Award from the Saginaw Bay Chapter of Phi Delta Kappa. In 1994 she was honored with the Earl L. Warrick Award for Excellence in Research from SVSU and she was recognized by the Michigan Association of Governing Boards of State Universities as a distinguished professor in 1995.

Elaine C. Stephens

Elaine C. Stephens, Professor of Teacher Education, Saginaw Valley State University, is a former classroom teacher, reading consultant, and professional development specialist. An active contributor to the profession, she presents at national and state conferences, is in frequent demand as an in-service speaker, and has written more than 40 publications. With Jean Brown and Lela Phillips, she co-authored the textbook, *Toward Literacy: Theory and Applications for Teaching Writing in the Content Areas*, (1993, Wadsworth Publishers). She also co-edited two teacher resource books, *Two Way Street: Integrating Reading and Writing in the Middle Schools* and *Two Way Street: Integrating Reading and Writing in the Secondary Schools* with Jean E. Brown and Barbara Quirk. She and Dr. Brown have a second textbook, *Literature for Young Adults Sharing the Connections,* 1995, from Wadsworth Publishers. She, Dr. Brown, and Dr. Janet Rubin are also the co-authors of *Learning About the Holocaust . . . Literature and Other Resources* from Library Professional Publications, Fall, 1995 and *Images from the Holocaust*, a literature anthology will be published in July 1996. She and Dr. Brown are currently writing a classroom practices book for the National Council of Teachers of English entitled *United in Diversity: Multicultural Young Adult Literature*. Currently, she is director of professional development for the Greater Saginaw Valley Regional Education Consortium and she is president of the Michigan Association of Colleges of Education. She is the 1992 recipient of the Franc A. Landee Award for Excellence in Teaching and was recognized by the Michigan Association of Governing Boards of State Universities for distinguished teaching and extraordinary contributions to higher education in 1993. Other recognition accorded her includes the 1990 Phi Delta Kappa Leadership Award from the Saginaw Bay Chapter and the PRAISE Award of Distinction for work with the Michigan Reading Association.